DESIGN AND TYPOGRAPHY
in easy steps

Sally Hughes

COMPUTER STEP

In easy steps is an imprint of Computer Step
Southfield Road . Southam
Warwickshire CV33 OFB . England

Tel: 01926 817999 Fax: 01926 817005
http://www.computerstep.com

Notice of Liability

Every effort has been made to ensure that this book contains accurate
and current information. However, Computer Step and the author shall
not be liable for any loss or damage suffered by readers as a result of
any information contained herein.

Trademarks

All trademarks are acknowledged as belonging to their respective
companies.

Acknowledgements

All photographs in this book are taken by R.H.Deahl.

Printed and bound in the United Kingdom

ISBN 1-84078-004-5

Contents

Chapter One

Starting your design

Design is a complex process. Dividing this process into simple steps and working from basic principles will help you work through this complexity. You will want to reconsider your decisions throughout the process to assess their effect.

What is design?

Design is a process. Applying this process correctly to text and graphics will improve the communication of your material and help readers to recall your message.

Whatever you put on your pages carries a message. Taking time to consider, test and improve your designs will help readers better understand, make them more receptive to the message and keep them interested.

Steps to follow

These are the steps which make up the design process. You will not always follow them in this order, nor will every one apply to every type of publication:

- *Understand your audience.* Who will read this publication and what is it intended to do? Will it inform them, intrigue them, annoy or remind them?

- *Decide on an appropriate format.* Is this publication a report, a poster, a pamphlet or a book? (See pages 16–19.) Alternatively, have you considered presenting the material as a web site? (See Chapter Eleven.)

- *Obtain and read the text carefully.* Printed communication is usually based on the written word. Does it address the audience in the correct style and level of English? Does it convey the message clearly and concisely? If the answer is No, then editing is needed, either by you, the author or an editor.

- *Create roughs.* These are quick sketches which indicate roughly where the text and graphics will appear on the page and how the text will be assigned to individual pages. If the publication will be printed on two sides, design the facing page spreads as a single entity. Draw your rough pages in approximately the correct format. See pages 26–27.

- *Obtain, edit and adjust the graphics.* Photographs, diagrams and illustrations will need to be chosen from existing sources or commissioned. Indicate on the rough sketches where they will appear. See Chapter Nine, *Graphics in your designs.*

 HANDY TIP Test your formats on a single page of text to see how the various styles work together.

- *Work out an appropriate format for each of the types of text.* Choose the font, typesize and alignment for the main paragraphs, any headings and other text such as quotations and captions, page numbers, headers and footers.

- *Convert your format ideas and rough sketches to the computer layout program.* This is where many inexperienced designers start, but without the preliminary steps you will make incorrect typographic decisions. The layout of text will take longer and more corrections will need to be made at a later stage.

- *Test and refine.* Print out the pages regularly as you lay them out and integrate graphics. Look critically at them yourself and show them to friends and colleagues for their opinion. Amend your design in response to your review and their comments.

- *Know when to stop.* This process can continue for some time, but eventually you will need to send the publication for printing. Don't let authors, editors and others bombard you with last minute changes to content. Set a deadline for these several days before you plan to finally prepare the camera-ready copy or send the files for printing.

Your work environment

Although good design can be created anywhere, you will turn out better results if you have good quality computer equipment, software and a reasonable amount of space.

Computer equipment

The computer needs to be fast enough (processing speed) to show any changes you make to the typography and design. Most new computers these days offer processing speeds in excess of what is needed to display your pages quickly and accurately.

Monitor

The size of your monitor is probably more important for design purposes than whether it displays colour. Colours, as they will appear on printed materials, are inaccurately displayed on computer screens. However, it is important to see as much of the page area you are designing as possible, and at 100% size or, in cases where work demands accurate attention to small detail, at higher magnification. Screens wider than 17 inches in diameter will make your work easier and quicker.

Printer

Printers come in diverse shapes and sizes, but the main consideration for design and typographic work is whether the printer uses the page description language, PostScript, which instructs your printer what to print. Although more expensive, a PostScript printer will provide a more accurate hard copy, because PostScript ensures that your work looks exactly the same on a 75dpi (dots per inch) monitor as printed on your own 300/600 dpi laser printer, or reproduced by a photosetting bureau on a high resolution image-setter. PostScript printers also allow your layout software to offer a wider range of facilities (eg, separating your files into printing ink colours) than those available in non-PostScript printers.

Scanner

A scanner translates flat artwork and photographs into digital files which can be added to your publications, then used for positioning and cropping on the pages. For high quality publications, these scans will be replaced before printing by higher resolution scans produced by your printer or service bureau.

...cont'd

 Computer Step publish books on all the major software packages in this same series.

Software

Essential software for any design and typography is a page layout program, such as Adobe PageMaker or QuarkXPress. You will also need word processing software for entering and manipulating the text quickly and easily and image processing software to prepare graphics files. Software, such as Adobe Illustrator, may be useful if you are planning to produce your own illustrations. In addition to digital fonts, you may want to acquire Adobe Type Manager which manages PostScript fonts (eg, adding fonts to or removing them from your system, and helping to display fonts more accurately on screen).

Space

Your actual layout work will be done on computer equipment which will take up space on your desk. If possible, you should also have another flat surface on which to display the printed pages. This will allow you to see the pages as your readers will see them and you will get a better impression of whether the design communicates your message.

Other equipment

Plain paper (A4), pencils, felt-tip pens and a ruler are all necessary for the sketching work which is an essential prerequisite for design.

Commercial printers

If you plan to use a commercial printer to reproduce your publications, contact your printer and get to know them. Their advice will be invaluable in constructing your page layout files and they will be able to help you avoid expensive mistakes.

Using contrast in your design

Contrast between the elements in your design will gain and retain your reader's attention. Used effectively, it makes your pages interesting, whilst also clarifying your message. The juxtaposition of different elements on your pages can involve size, position, weight and shape.

Size

Large variations of size are most effectively used in advertisements and posters.

Shape

Contrast in shape can be achieved by varying the typefaces used and in careful use of different graphic shapes on the page. A change in typeface for headings introduces shape contrast in reports and booklets, while changes in strong graphic shapes are probably more appropriate in posters.

 Variation in size for headings in reports and booklets must be chosen in relation to the look of the pages as a whole.

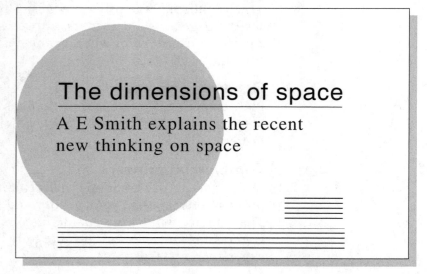

The dimensions of space

A E Smith explains the recent new thinking on space

Weight

A contrast in weight can be achieved by changing the typeface. Alternatively, in a single typeface, the weight of characters can be changed. Most commonly, bold is applied to darken the characters.

Our**Time**

OurTime

Alignment and position

Within a single page or in a poster, varying the alignment and position of design elements can produce considerable contrast. You can also use position contrast from page to page within a single document.

Test any design which involves more than one type of contrast with colleagues, to check that you have enough contrast to achieve the effect but not so much that the message is difficult to read and comprehend.

A man for our times

The story of A E Smith

Balance as a design principle

Once you are sure your design includes contrast, you will want to look at the page or pages to ensure there is a balance in its overall appearance.

At its simplest, this means that a heavy dark shape needs some counteracting shape to leave the page balanced as a whole. Just as contrast is easy to see in a poster, so balance is easier to achieve in this freer format.

This large grey shape is balanced by the smaller, blacker shape in the bottom right corner

This long passage of text is balanced by the smaller passage in the top right corner

Balance is equally important in reports, booklets and other paged literature. However, balance must be achieved within the stringent typographic constraints and with careful consideration of your reader. Use subtle effects and apply your balance across the double-page spread.

Balance facing pages as if they were a single unit. This creates cohesion in your document.

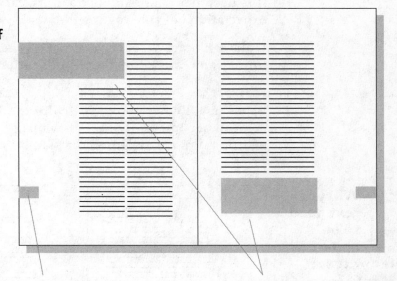

Page numbers that are mirrored across the double-page spread provide a balance. Reversing the number against a grey shape also provides contrast to the text.

Graphics can provide balance to your pages. Although not exactly opposite each other, these two rectangles balance the pages as a whole.

Types of publication

Newspapers, direct mail literature, correspondence, business documents, information booklets and both fiction and nonfiction books make up our daily diet of printed material. Your publication will be read against this vast and bewildering array and needs to fit with existing publication conventions. A report looks like a report because of the way it is designed and readers open its pages with certain expectations of the way it will be laid out.

Unless you are an experienced designer, work within the limitations offered by these publication types.

Reports

Pages usually have one wide column. Occasionally, this column occupies only part of the page to leave room for an additional narrow column, or side headings.

 HANDY TIP

Will your text need to be updated regularly? If so, consider using a ring-binder and sending out the new pages for the readers to add themselves.

The A4 documents are easy to produce since practically all printers take this paper size as standard and a range of simple binding methods are available for the single sheets. Publications in this format are inexpensive to reproduce by photocopying. However, full printing may prove economical if you want more than (about) 500 copies.

Printing makes many more formats available and offers a range of binding options. Using a non-A4 page size and a more permanent binding method such as staples or perfect binding will give your publication a more professional appearance.

Marketing material

Low cost marketing material can be produced from your office. Keep the text short and succinct; use interesting and appropriate photographs. Folded A2 will give you four pages of A4, which provides plenty of space for description of your company and its products or services. Don't forget the contact information, including your e-mail and web site if there is one.

Information leaflets (folded A4)

Folded leaflets can be economical and effective. The folds help define different areas of the text. Experiment with different fold directions to see which fits best with your material.

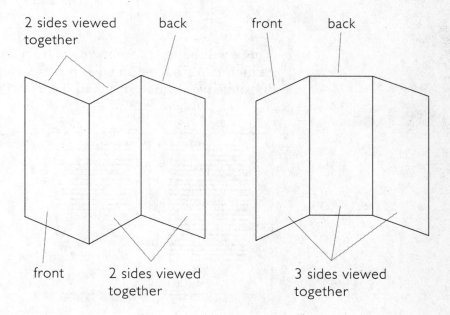

2 sides viewed together — back — front — back

front — 2 sides viewed together — 3 sides viewed together

Choosing a format

Your decision on page dimensions will be decided by the type of publication. The most common format in the office is A4, usually used in portrait (tall) orientation.

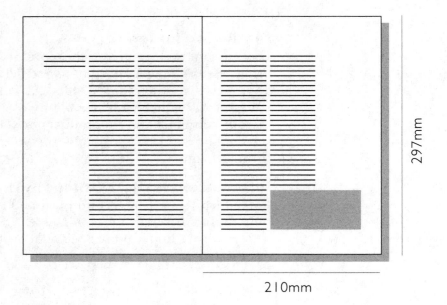

There will be times when you want a smaller format. A5 (which is A4 halved in size) offers a compact and inexpensive format for small information booklets.

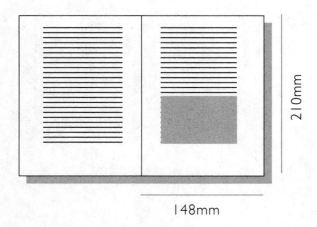

If you are using a commercial printer to reproduce your publication, you can easily move away from these commonly used and therefore familiar formats. Other page sizes offer interesting design opportunities and will help your publications stand out against the more usual A4 or A5 formats.

Square

Any page which has the same height and width is of interest. People find the shape pleasing and are intrigued by its regularity. The use of strongly uneven margins provides a strong contrast and makes the pages even more interesting. Keep the overall size small, since storage of publications which are wide and tall is difficult and you may find your publication is relegated to an out-of-the-way place and forgotten because it does not fit neatly on to bookshelves or in filing cabinets.

 Wide margins give a sense of luxury to your pages.

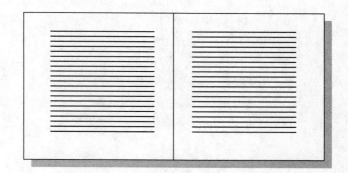

Landscape orientation

A landscape orientation is any page which is wider than it is high. This format provides the opportunity for more columns across the page and is used well with photographic illustrations as most of these are also landscape. However, these books are wide when open. They are not a useful format for technical documents or user manuals as they can be unwieldy.

Looking at your material

You will already have decided what type of publication you are creating and may have chosen a format. The next step is making sure you are familiar with your material. Since design is about communication, you must be sure you understand the message of your material and have a clear idea of the audience it is intended for.

Read the text carefully to make sure that:

- the material is complete, including graphics and captions;

- the writing is clear and concise;

- the style and content is appropriate to the audience.

Heading levels

When you are happy with the text, look at it again: this time, impose a structure on the message. Initially, it should be easy to see headings in the text, but it may be necessary to work out levels in the headings. Try to use no more than three.

How electricity is made ——————— Heading level 1 introduces the main subject

The electricity in our homes is made in power stations. There are three main types.

Power from water ——————— Heading level 2 introduces one of the three categories of power station

A hydro-electric power station uses falling water to make electricity. The water rushes down a pipe from a reservoir.

Turbines ——————— Heading level 3 provides divisions within level two text

At the bottom of the pipe, water pushes past the turbine blades, which turns them.

Special treatments

Are there any parts of the text which should be presented as bulleted or numbered points; as a table; emphasized between rules; in a box? Mark them on your hard copy and keep them in mind when you are deciding on the typography and page layout grid.

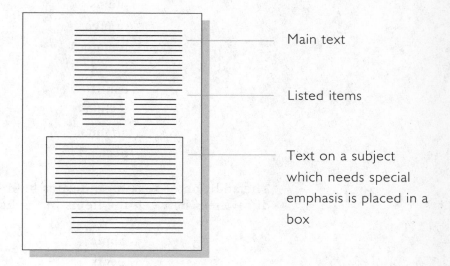

Main text

Listed items

Text on a subject which needs special emphasis is placed in a box

Graphics

Decide how the graphics, if any, will best enhance the text. Should they be treated as simple photographs with captions laid alongside, or as elements on the page which enhance its appearance? Will the captions provide an opportunity for presenting information in short digestible chunks, rather than within the main text?

Check back

Design is a repetitive process. Once you have completed these steps, go back over them again to make sure that revisions have not adversely affected earlier design ideas. As you continue on through the design and production process, you may need to alter your ideas further. This is a natural part of the design process. Do not be disheartened – your publications will benefit from this repetition.

Using space in your design

Used to group the text, space can indicate similarity and difference in meaning. The structure in the list below is difficult to understand as there is no change in spacing.

apples

pears

plums

oranges

tomatoes

carrots

cauliflower

walnuts

almonds

pecans

The addition of spacing indicates both similarity and differences between the items in the list.

apples

pears

plums

oranges

tomatoes

carrots

cauliflower

walnuts

almonds

pecans

Using space in headings

Subtle changes in space can be used to indicate levels of headings and provide emphasis to separate them from the remaining text.

This text called Lorem Ipsum is used to work out the design of text. Since you cannot read, or make sense of it, you are forced to look at the design and are not distracted by the content.

Lorem ipsum

Dolor sit amet, consectetuer adipiscing elit, sed diam nonummy nibh.

Ut wisi enim

Dd minim veniam, quis nostrud exerci tation ullamcorper suscipit lobortis nisl ut aliquip ex ea commodo consequat.

When you space a heading, make sure it remains visually attached to its related paragraph. Add more space above the heading than below it.

Dolor sit amet, consectetuer adipiscing elit, sed diam nonummy nibh.

Ut wisi enim

Dd minim veniam, quis nostrud exerci tation ullamcorper suscipit lobortis nisl ut aliquip ex ea commodo consequat.

This heading has equal spacing above and below. It does not look related to the following text.

Dolor sit amet, consectetuer adipiscing elit, sed diam nonummy nibh.

Ut wisi enim

Dd minim veniam, quis nostrud exerci tation ullamcorper suscipit lobortis nisl ut aliquip ex ea commodo consequat.

This heading has more space above (2.5 mm) than below (1 mm) it. It now relates to the following text.

Using appearance in your design

Similarity and differences in typefaces (ie, their appearance) can bring out the similarities and differences in the meaning of the content. Variation in typeface, weight and size, combined to give a distinct appearance, can be used to distinguish the various functions of text in any document.

apples	apples
pears	pears
plums	plums
oranges	oranges
tomatoes	**tomatoes**
carrots	**carrots**
cauliflower	**cauliflower**

Choose an appropriate amount of change

How much change in appearance you create to distinguish your headings will depend on how complicated the rest of the page is. If the page is simple, you should be able to create the required distinction with only two of these options. A complex page may need a significant change of point size, spacing and typeface appearance.

Lorem ipsum

Dolor sit amet, consectetuer adipiscing elit, sed diam nonummy nibh.

Ut wisi enim

Dd minim veniam, quis nostrud exerci tation ullamcorper suscipit lobortis nisl ut aliquip ex ea commodo consequat.

Differences in appearance can also indicate differences of function in a document. Captions, usually relatively short in length, can be set apart from the main text by changing the typeface to italic or sans serif.

Using alignment in your design

Alignment and position of text on the page can bring out differences. Here the list is presented in categories which are defined by their position on the page. The line adds subtle emphasis to the groups.

apples	tomatoes	walnuts
pears	carrots	almonds
plums	cauliflower	pecans
oranges		

Page design

Looking at the design of the page as a whole, you can use position of the text blocks on the page and a change in alignment to distinguish text.

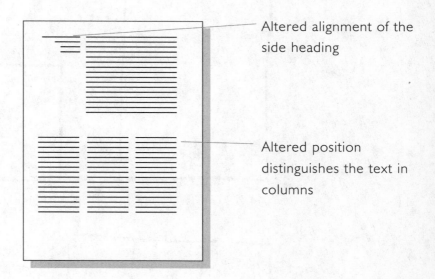

Altered alignment of the side heading

Altered position distinguishes the text in columns

Since differences in appearance affect the way readers comprehend text, you must ensure that similar text receives a uniform typographic treatment. Readers will interpret any unintended differences as having a meaning.

Sketching your ideas

Before you start working on the computer, you should sketch your designs on paper. This will help you see the overall effect of your ideas, decide quickly which ones might work and make the process of interpreting your design on the computer easier.

These rough sketches should be relatively simple. On blank paper, using a pencil or fine felt-tip pen, try to show position, alignment and the relative weight of design elements.

Page sketches

A simple rectangle will represent the page. Draw the format accurately since the proportions will affect your design decisions.

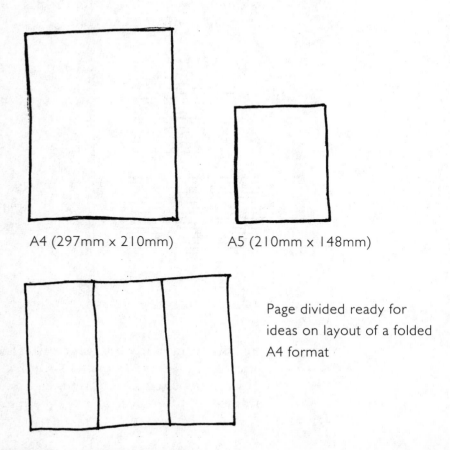

A4 (297mm x 210mm)   A5 (210mm x 148mm)

Page divided ready for ideas on layout of a folded A4 format

Text sketches

You will come up with your own style for these sketches. Make sure you show position, alignment and the relative weight and size of the text in some way. Here are some ideas on how you could do this:

Thin, black felt-tipped pens are very useful for indicating text lines.

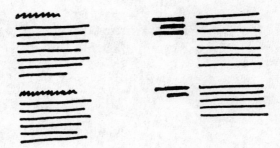

Document sketches

A full, long document with many pages can be shown with a series of pages laid out in order, and showing which is left and right if appropriate.

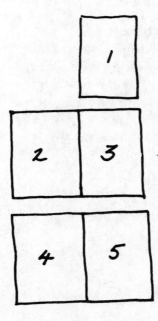

This rough sketch indicates page numbers and page spreads. You can add notes on the content and approximate position of graphics, headers, footers and page numbers. These sketches are also useful for working out sections, chapters and correct pages for preliminary material.

Managing design

The design and production of effective publications requires careful management. As a process, it involves many roles from authors, editors, designers and illustrators to computer operators and printers. Different people could be involved, or it may be just you carrying out these tasks. In either case, the flow of work from first draft to finished product must be kept on schedule and usually to a budget.

Project manager

As the manager of the project you will need:

- a realistic schedule for the entire project;

- interim deadlines to help keep the project on time;

- a knowledge of what is required at each stage;

- an overview of the budget;

- a knowledge of the cost of design decisions.

If you are responsible for design and production of publications, but are not in a position to manage the process effectively, you will need to work with your manager to obtain co-operation in achieving these aims.

A final hint

Keep one portfolio of your work, and another of publications designed by others. These collections will increase your design ability and knowledge. Choose ones which you like, examples of unusual design solutions and also examples of poor design so that you can avoid similar mistakes. Designers borrow and adapt existing designs.

Typing your text

The key strokes used to enter text on a computer can affect the typography. Understanding and care during typing will help you achieve good typography in later stages of publication production.

Covers

Chapter Two

Spacing after full stops

Whether you or someone else types the text, the keys pressed must give the correct character and result in the correct spacing for the typography. This is self-evident for the 26 character alphabet which makes up words, but it is equally true for many of the typographic symbols, special characters and the spaces which make up the rest of the written language.

Although many typists still place two spaces after a full stop, this is incorrect for text which will be set according to typographic rules. The double-spacing combines with the space created by the full stop to give a wide gap between the end of one sentence and the beginning of the next. Press the spacebar once only after a full stop.

Print regularly as you are laying out pages. You will see aspects of the design that would be missed on screen. You will use more paper but have fewer mistakes.

Holes appear in the text where two spaces have been typed

Print regularly as you are laying out pages. You will see aspects of the design that would be missed on screen. You will use more paper but have fewer mistakes.

A single space designates a new sentence but does not create a white space in the text

Spacing after paragraphs

Typists often insert an additional line between contiguous paragraphs to distinguish them from each other. As they reach the end of one paragraph, they press the Return key twice and then start typing the next paragraph.

The area of Mexico is approximately two million square kilometres. It forms a link between the north American continent and tropical Central South America. ¶
¶
Landscapes of Mexico can be divided into three main types: mountains, coastal plains and peninsulas. ¶
¶

Incorrect double-return to space paragraphs

 You can quickly remove the extra paragraphs and spaces using the Find and Replace facility in your word processing software.

This additional line (which the computer 'sees' as an additional paragraph even though it contains no words) makes adjusting the paragraph spacing difficult or impossible. Paragraph spacing is an important aspect of designing your message for the reader as we will see in Chapter Four.

Always prepare text for design so that the paragraphs are separated by only one Return key stroke.

The area of Mexico is approximately two million square kilometres. It forms a link between the north American continent and tropical Central South America. ¶
Landscapes of Mexico can be divided into three main types: mountains, coastal plains and peninsulas. ¶

Correct single return to create the paragraph

Typing and using tabs efficiently

Most word processing and page layout programs display **small arrows where tab keys have been typed. Displaying these small arrows will help you to work out where and how many tabs have been typed if someone else has typed the text for you to use.**

Tabs are markers set in the text which allow the typist to jump the cursor to a preset position. They are used to position text (such as figures in tables) accurately in columns. Most computer software programs provide default tabs set in predetermined positions so that typists only need to press the tab key to move the cursor.

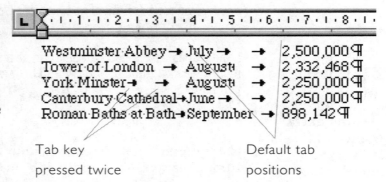

Tab key
pressed twice

Default tab
positions

These default tab positions are rarely in the correct position to line up all table entries, so typists press the tab key twice or three times so that the entries do line up. This addition of extra tab key strokes causes problems if text is altered – eg, if the typeface, point size or the line length changes. The text no longer lines up and the extra tab key strokes push the alignment out even further. They then have to be removed.

Westminster Abbey → July → → 2,500,000 ¶
Tower of London → August → → 2,332,468 ¶
York Minster → → August → 2,250,000 ¶
Canterbury Cathedral → June → 2,250,000 ¶
Roman Baths at Bath → September → 898,142 ¶

Here, the increased point size causes the
tab key to push out the text alignment

When typing tabbed text, separate each column entry with a single tab key. This will create text which will be simple and quick to align in columns after the correct typeface, point size, and line length is applied.

```
Westminster Abbey  →   July→2,500,000¶
Tower of London→August  →   2,332,468¶
York Minster  →   August  →   2,250,000¶
Canterbury Cathedral →  June→2,250,000¶
Roman Baths at Bath  →  September→898,142¶
```

Single tab keys separate each entry although they do not yet align correctly

	20	40	60	80	100
Westminster Abbey		July			2,500,000
Tower of London		August			2,332,468
York Minster		August			2,250,000
Canterbury Cathedral		June			2,250,000
Roman Baths at Bath		September			898,142

Text in a page layout program with the correct typeface and type size applied

Tab markers positioned to correctly align the columns

Typing correct characters

Typing the correct characters may seem self-evident, but it is easy to confuse letters of the alphabet and to key in the wrong punctuation. Also, there are some conventions, common in typing, which are never seen in typography.

Confusing letters and numerals

Most of the twenty–six characters in the alphabet and the ten numerals have unique shapes and cannot be confused with each other. However, the few which can be confused require careful attention because a switch may not be obvious in one typeface but will create glaring errors in another. Check your typed text carefully to ensure that it shows the correct characters.

You may want to change the typeface temporarily since this can help you decide whether the character is an 'el' or a number one.

In Helvetica, the letter 'el' and the capital 'i' are very similar and could be mistaken for the number one. The number 'zero' and a capital 'o' are similar shapes in all typefaces.

Dashes and hyphens

Many typists enter hyphens when they should type one of two other lines or dashes, both of which are longer than the hyphen.

The em dash is a long line used to indicate a pause in reading. It can be used instead of a colon:

> This is the end — there is no more.

An en dash is used to indicate a duration of time or to link two parts of a group.

> September – October

Most word processing programs provide ways to enter em and en dashes.

Quotation marks

Quotation marks indicate speech and inserts from other texts. Typographic styles vary between countries and, depending on the conventions, quotations may be double or single marks. Most keyboards show only one key for these different single and double marks. Some word processing programs will automatically substitute the straight quote for typographic quotes. However, it is better to use the correct key strokes rather than rely on this substitution which does not always carry over into page layout programs. You may need to use your Help files to find out which are the correct key strokes.

“ ”   ‘ ’

Ellipsis

An ellipsis is a series of three dots which indicate that something is missing from the text, or that there is something to follow. Many people type three full stops, but the spacing is different for a true ellipsis which is a single character. An ellipsis in a sentence is preceded and followed by a space.

HANDY TIP

You can tell whether you have an ellipsis or three separate dots by placing the cursor to the right of the three dots. If you backspace to remove the character and the three dots disappear in one go, you have removed an ellipsis. Choose Undo to replace the character.

• • •   • • •

The second group of dots is a true ellipsis

Virgule and solidus

A virgule is used to separate alternative words.

and/or

A solidus is used to separate the upper and lower numbers in a fraction. It is more slanted than the virgule.

$\frac{1}{2}$

Special characters

Special characters are those characters which cannot be typed directly. They may be accented characters, special numerals and ligatures amongst many possibilities.

Accented characters

Most common accented characters, such as

é   è   ü   î   ñ   ç   å   ä   ô

can be typed using a combination of key strokes. If you do not know how to type them, you should find out using your software Help files.

Special numerals

Most numerals provided with standard fonts are designed to fit easily into tables so that it is easy to read across the lines of type. If your text contains numbers mixed with the words, you may want to consider purchasing a special font containing old style numbers. These numerals are designed to sit above and below the line of text and to fit well with the alphabet characters.

1 2 3 4 5 6 7 8 9 0 ____ Old style numbers fit well with the
ascenders and descenders of text

Ligatures

A ligature is a single character used instead of letter pairs because it gives a better fit.

Ligatures are usually inserted using a search and replace facility. You will need to find out what key strokes are required for the ligature and then replace the two characters for the single ligature.

fi fi ——————— The dot of the 'i' and the top of the 'l'
fl fl   clash with the end of the 'f' unless they are
created as a single entity

Chapter Three

Understanding typefaces

Typefaces are the building blocks of your publications. Their appearance affects the way your words are represented. Understanding how this works will help you choose the right typefaces for your publications.

Covers

Aspects of a typeface

A typeface is the collection of distinct letters and other characters available for use in printing your text. Typefaces differ in their letter shapes and the range of faces offer infinite variation. However, some standard parts of the letters are universal.

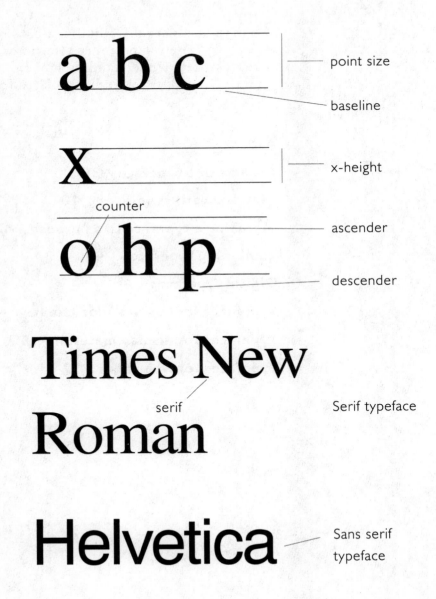

point size

baseline

x-height

counter

ascender

descender

Times New Roman

serif

Serif typeface

Helvetica

Sans serif typeface

Variation in stroke weight

Some typefaces show a strong contrast between the stroke or lines which make up the letter shape. The variation in the lines is a characteristic of the typeface. Some are extreme, others show no variation and are said to be monoline.

variation in stroke width creates a strong contrast within the letter shapes

o e l

no variation in the stroke width creates a monoline letter shape

o e l

Enlarging letters or numerals to 36 points or larger will help you to see the distinct shapes of your typefaces.

Stress

Where there is a variation in stroke weight, the place where the weight changes in the counters gives a stress to the letter. Many letters show a backwards slant to the stress while a few have an upright stress.

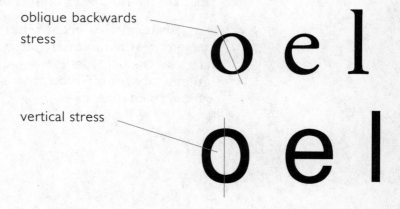

oblique backwards stress

o e l

vertical stress

o e l

Sans and serif typefaces

One of the most obvious differences between typefaces is the shape and presence or absence of a serif. Helvetica and Arial are sans serif typefaces, Times and Palatino are serif typefaces. All four are commonly found on computer systems.

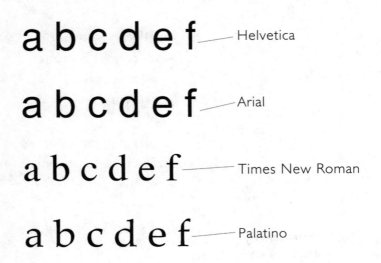

— Helvetica

— Arial

— Times New Roman

— Palatino

You can buy additional fonts to increase your choice of sans and serif typefaces.

Serif

In material intended for continuous reading, such as reports, the serif is said to help a reader's eye follow along a line of text. This effect makes a seriffed typeface the usual choice for such publications.

The additional area of the letter created by the serif makes a page of text using a seriffed typeface denser and darker than a sans serif typeface would appear. Text can be lightened by adding more space between the lines. This is covered in chapter 4.

When to use sans serif typeface

Sans serif typefaces can be effective in headings, shorter pieces of text and in tables where clarity of character outline is important.

Lorem ipsum

Duis autem vel eum iriure dolor in hendrerit in vulputate velit esse molestie consequat, vel illum dolore eu feugiat nulla facilisis at vero eros et accumsan et iusto.

Helvetica is appropriate to use for subheadings and short pieces of text, but it is difficult to read for extended text.

The layout grid is displayed on screen to help you place text and graphics on the page. It does not print. Hiding the grid will give you some idea of how the printed page will look.

When to use a serif typeface

Seriffed typefaces are used in continuous text where ease of reading is important. Words hang together better when set in a serif typeface:

Space is where the gas Helium was first found. It is the only element to be discovered on the Sun before it was discovered on Earth. Norman Lockyer, a civil servant, who founded London's Science Museum found it there on 28th October 1868, when he pointed his telescope at the Sun and examined the light with a spectroscope. In the spectrum of the solar prominence he was surprised to see a curious yellow line.

Matching a typeface to a purpose

One reason why there are so many typefaces to choose from is that each is designed for a particular purpose.

For example, Times New Roman is a compact typeface designed for use in newspapers. You can get more characters in a line of Times New Roman than in less compact faces. This makes it a good choice for newsletters. ITC Officina is also a compact typeface.

ITC Officina is a compact typeface which is very useful for setting short lines of type in newsletters.

Times New Roman is a compact typeface which is very useful for setting short lines of type in newsletters.

Elaborate typefaces

Script typefaces are commonly available on computer systems. Their elaborate letter shapes make them suitable for elegant invitations but they are difficult to read in extended amounts of text and are of limited use.

You are cordially invited to a celebration on 21st June

Work-horse typefaces

Palatino and New Century Schoolbook are work-horse typefaces. They can be used again and again for everyday reports and correspondence. Their well-designed letter shapes mean they are pleasing to read but do not call attention to themselves. The message gets through.

Avoid any typefaces with startling letter shapes for continuous reading. The complex shapes attract attention to themselves and detract from the information.

REMEMBER **Keep a portfolio of interesting and appropriate use of typefaces. Try to name the typefaces or match them to ones on your computer.**

Palatino is a useful typeface for every day use.

New Century Schoolbook is also useful for every day use in reports and letters.

Get to know your typefaces

Spend some time getting to know the typefaces on your computer system so that they are not just names that you pick at random.

Type a short paragraph of three to four lines, an alphabet in upper and lower case and the numbers and punctuation symbols.

Highlight this text and apply the first typeface. Label the text with the font you have applied.

Copy the paragraph, paste it on the same page and then apply the next typeface. Again, label the text with the correct font. Continue applying the fonts in this manner on your system.

Print out the pages. Look at the fonts and then categorise them according to their stress, weight and serifs.

Combining typefaces

Take great care when including additional typefaces in your documents. Make every effort to express the content of the message with one typeface only. If you do add further typefaces, ensure they contrast with each other.

 Keep the number of typefaces in one document to a minimum: no more than two for your first publications.

Contrast in shape

Readers will spot the strong differences in shape easily and use them to interpret your message.

Frutiger and Bookman provide sufficient contrast.

Lorem ipsum — dolor sit amet consect adipiscing elit sed diam nonummy.

Baskerville Semibold and Arial provide a similar contrast.

Lorem ipsum
Dolor sit amet consect adipiscing elit set diam nonummy.

Watch out for the x-height

You may need to alter the point size of different typeface on the same line if they have widely different x-heights. In the example above, Baskerville is set in 24 points, while Arial is in 18 although the actual size of the letters would indicate they are in the same point size.

Different typefaces for different functions

Different typefaces can be used for different functions in a document. Choose one main typeface for the body text and use it extensively in the main paragraphs and low level headings.

Helium ——————————————— Heading Times New Roman, 24 point

Space is where the gas Helium was first found. It is the only element to be discovered on the Sun before it was ——— Body text Times New Roman 12 point

discovered on Earth. Norman Lockyer, a civil servant, who founded London's Science Museum found it there on 28th October 1868, when he pointed his telescope at the Sun and examined the light with a spectroscope.

A yellow line ———————————— Subheading Times New Roman, 14 point bold

In the spectrum of the solar prominence he was surprised to see a curious yellow line.

Navigational aids

Choose another contrasting typeface for the navigational aids such as page numbers, headers and footers, and section breaks. This second typeface could also be used for the captions or figure titles. Helvetica is used in the examples below.

A history of the elements ——— Header, 11 pt

34 ——— Page no's 14 pt

The spectrum of Helium was ——— Captions, 12 pt
first seen by Norman Lockyer.

Digital typefaces

Understanding technical aspects of computer typefaces will help you work out any problems you may have using fonts. Digital typefaces are composed of two main parts: the computer file which displays the letter shapes on the computer screen (a bitmap file) and the file sent to the printer to print the corresponding letter.

These files are provided by font suppliers in different ways. The two main types are PostScript and TrueType.

PostScript fonts
The bitmap and printing files for these fonts are provided as separate entities and must both be present on your computer system.

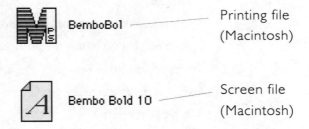

BemboBol ———— Printing file (Macintosh)

Bembo Bold 10 ———— Screen file (Macintosh)

TrueType fonts
These fonts provide the data for both screen and printing in one combined file. The advantage of this approach is that the files cannot be separated and lost.

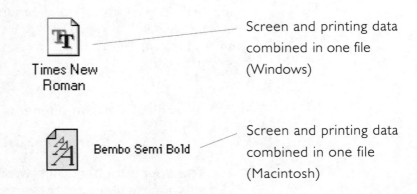

Times New Roman ———— Screen and printing data combined in one file (Windows)

Bembo Semi Bold ———— Screen and printing data combined in one file (Macintosh)

Character set

The character set of a typeface is the complete set of characters which the typeface offers. In standard fonts, such as Times New Roman shown below, this will include the full upper case and lower case alphabet, several accented letters, the numbers and the most commonly used punctuation symbols.

Most font foundries maintain web sites where you can browse for new typefaces. Some allow you to download a screen version so that you can test the typeface in your publication. You can then purchase the printing font.

a b c d e f g h i j k
A B C D E F G H I
1 2 3 4 5 6 7 8 9 0
, . / Õ ; [ ] - = ` ! @
£ $ % ^ & * ( ) _
{ } : Ó > ? < | \
Á ª # ¢ ∞ ¤ ¦ ¥ » ¼
Đ ≠ Ô Ò π ¿ ^ ¬ ´ Σ
Ï Œ § ∂ Ä © ú Δ û Å
É ¾ ÷ ≥ ≤ µ ~ ∫ √ •
À ® ò ñ   ï î

The character set will not necessarily include all the characters you need for your text. If necessary, these are available in a range of other fonts which you will have to purchase separately.

Choosing additional typefaces

If you are able to purchase additional typefaces, keep the following points in mind:

*   Purchase typefaces that complement the typefaces already on your computer system.

*   Purchase typefaces from an established foundry.

*   Don't accept copies of font software – this is illegal.

*   Check that the character set for your chosen typeface provides the characters you will need.

Typefaces for business documents

Ease of reading is the main consideration in choosing typefaces for business documents. In some organisations, the choice of typeface is prescribed, but often it is left up to individuals.

Typefaces for reports

Reports require readers' prolonged attention. In choosing a typeface, look for a serif typeface with an unfussy letter shape which is easy to read at 10, 12 and 14 points. Times New Roman is commonly used because it is often the default typeface and no one changes it, but there may be other more attractive typefaces on your computer, such as Garamond, Book Antiqua and Bookman. These familiar typefaces make for easy reading in extended amounts of text.

Space is where the gas Helium was first found. It is the only element to be discovered on the Sun before it was discovered on Earth. Norman Lockyer, a civil servant, who founded London's Science Museum, found it there on 28th October 1868, when he pointed his telescope at the Sun and examined the light with a spectroscope.

Garamond

Space is where the gas Helium was first found. It is the only element to be discovered on the Sun before it was discovered on Earth. Norman Lockyer, a civil servant, who founded London's Science Museum, found it there on 28th October 1868, when he pointed his telescope at the Sun and examined the light with a spectroscope.

Book Antiqua

Space is where the gas Helium was first found. It is the only element to be discovered on the Sun before it was discovered on Earth. Norman Lockyer, a civil servant, who founded London's Science Museum, found it there on 28th October 1868, when he pointed his telescope at the Sun and examined the light with a spectroscope.

Bookman

The typefaces you use in business reports and correspondence are an important part of the overall design image of your company.

Typefaces for letters and memos

Letters and memos require a typeface which will be easy to read, work well at 10 and 12 points and will fit with any logos, graphics or type already printed on the letterhead. Try out various typefaces in sample letters and see which you and your colleagues prefer. Agree a standard and then stick with it. Most word processing software allows you to set up templates which hold the preferred typeface.

Typefaces for faxes

Faxes require not only a typeface which is easy to read, but one which is robust – ie, it must remain easy to read when transmitted and printed on fax paper. Faxes are often photocopied and faxed again. Any typeface with delicate serifs or small counters will have lost its letter shapes after this treatment. Choose a typeface with a large x-height, distinct ascenders and descenders and large counters. New Century Schoolbook is a good example of a robust typeface.

New Century Schoolbook is a good example of a robust typeface.

Typefaces for display materials

The possibilities for creative work with type are greater in display materials. Posters and advertisements need to attract attention and unusual, eye-catching type is one way to achieve this.

Type carries a message. Never alter your text so completely that it is impossible to understand the message.

Choosing a typeface

A clean, clear outline to your letter shape is the best attribute to look for when selecting a typeface. Sans serif faces such as Arial and Gill Sans, or open, bold serif faces such as Book Antiqua and Bookman are good places to start. They will carry the message well at any point size and act as a foil to any graphics you might include. If these are not available on your system, you can stick with Helvetica and Palatino or Times New Roman.

Look here!   Arial

Look here!   Gill Sans

This is good   Book Antiqua

This is good   Bookman

Altered letter shape

Most software programs offer options for altering the letter shape, such as Bold and Italic. You could use these effects on text at 18 points and above, but use them sparingly as they make text difficult to read.

Bold *Italic*

Making a pattern

Repeating a letter, word or phrase can be an effective way to attract attention. The type becomes a pattern which reinforces your message. The typeface you choose for the pattern is less important because the message will be carried by other type, but this might be a place for more elaborate letter shapes.

A A A Absolutely
B B B Beautiful

Shaped text

Some computer graphics programs allow you to shape the text along a line. The type itself becomes a graphic.

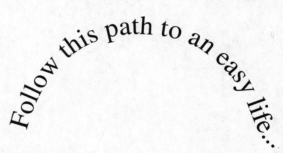

Reversing text

Reversing type is an effective way to create contrast, but you can also use this effect to create intrigue and surprise by adjusting the position of the reverse and the type.

ATTENTION

Try it
www.gotcha.com

Typefaces for web pages

 Choose typefaces with distinct letter shapes – large x-height, open counters and large ascenders and descenders – for easy screen reading.

Reading text on screen requires more concentration than reading on printed paper. For this reason, you should take even more care in choosing appropriate typefaces. If you want to specify the font your pages use, you will need to add GIF text to your pages. There is more about this on page 176.

Although you can use any typeface for your GIF web text, there are now a number of typefaces which are specifically designed for use on web pages:

Minion Web
Designed by Adobe, this typeface comes bundled with Microsoft Internet Explorer. It is suitable for both text and display typography.

Mezz Web
This typeface works well for display typography.

Chapter Four

Spacing your text

Good use of space between words, sentences and paragraphs will make your text easy to read and help readers to better understand your message.

Covers

Spacing between lines of type

The white space between lines of type is called leading. The term comes from the small strips of lead which were inserted between the pieces of metal type when type was positioned by hand. Leading is measured in points from the baseline of one line of type to the baseline of the subsequent line.

Lorem ipsum dolor sit
amet consectetuer
adipiscing elitsed diam
non nibh euismod

Leading is space between baselines of text

 Similar paragraphs should always have the same leading. If you have to change leading, adjust it for all similar paragraphs.

Leading can also be referred to as interline spacing. Word processing programs allow you to control interline spacing using single, 1.5 and double line spacing. These settings are less effective than the more gradual leading controls in page layout programs.

Lorem ipsum dolor sit
amet consectetuer
adipiscing elitsed diam
non nibh euismod

Single line spacing

Lorem ipsum dolor sit

amet consectetuer

adipiscing elitsed diam

non nibh euismod

1.5 line spacing

This difference is one of the main reasons for using page layout programs rather than word processing programs when designing and laying out documents.

Auto leading

Most page layout software applies default leading based on the chosen point size of the text. Usually, the leading is 120% of the text, so that 10 point text has 12 points of leading applied to it. As the text point size increases, so does the leading.

Lorem ipsum dolor sit amet consectetuer adipiscing elitsed diam non nibh euismod

Auto leading gives 2 points of space

Lorem ipsum dolor sit amet consectetuer adipiscing

Auto leading for 18 points gives 21.6 points of leading

Absolute leading

Absolute leading is the line spacing chosen by you and not by the software. You can choose more subtle changes in leading than the default 120%. As we will see in the next pages, you should consider more than just the typeface point size when you select the leading.

Lorem ipsum dolor sit amet consectetuer adipiscing

Absolute leading of 20 points provides the right amount of spacing between lines

Choosing leading

When choosing leading for your type, you will want to start by considering the point size of the text. Other aspects of type affect the leading individually and also interact with each other. These pages provide advice on how to choose leading for your text.

Design is a repetitive process. Test your leading choice to see if it is easy to read. Readjust if necessary.

Point size

As the size of your text gets larger, it needs more leading. This is so that the lines of type do not overlap. The amount you add will depend on other factors.

Peter Piper picked a peck of pickled pepper ————— 12 points on 14 leading

Peter Piper picked a peck of pickled pepper ————— 18 points on 20 leading

Peter Piper picked a peck of pickled pepper ————— 24 points on 25.5 leading

Negative leading

Some headings can be set with negative leading. This is spacing that is less than the point size of the text.

Peter Piper picks Peppers ————— 36 points on 35.5 leading

Typeface

Different letter shapes require different spacing between the lines of type. For example, a typeface like Helvetica which has a large x-height will require more space than one like Times New Roman which has a small x-height.

Getting to know the look of the typefaces on your system will help you when making decisions on leading.

Red lorries, yellow lorries
Blue lollies, orange lollies

Helvetica, 14 points on 17.5 leading

Red lorries, yellow lorries
Blue lollies, orange lollies

Times New Roman, 14 points on 15.5 leading

The size of ascenders and descenders in relation to the x-height of the letters affect the amount of leading needed. In addition, some typefaces have large counters. In a block of text these give a lighter appearance than other typefaces with small counters. This intrinsic white space will affect the amount of leading.

Line length

The length of a line of text affects the reader's ability to read and comprehend your message. The longer the line, the more difficult it is for the reader to find the beginning of the next line quickly and easily. Leading can help this process by spacing out the lines and making it easy to continue reading fluently.

Lorem ipsum dolor sit amet, consectetuer adipiscing elit, sed diam nonummy nibh euismod tincidunt ut laoreet dolore magna aliquam erat volutpat. Ut wisi enim ad minim veniam, quis nost-rud exerci tation ullamcorper suscipit lobortis nisl ut aliquip ex ea commodo consequat.

With 10 point text, 15 points leading is necessary because of the length of line

Lorem ipsum dolor sit amet, consectetuer adipiscing elit, sed diam nonummy nibh euismod tincidunt ut laoreet dolore magna aliquam erat volutpat. Ut wisi enim ad minim veniam, quis nost-rud exerci tation ullamcorper suscipit lobortis nisl ut aliquip ex ea commodo consequat.

10 point text with 13.5 points of leading for this shorter line

Lorem ipsum dolor sit amet, consectetuer adipiscing elit, sed diam nonummy nibh euismod tincidunt ut laoreet dolore magna aliquam erat volutpat. Ut wisi enim ad minim veniam, quis nost-rud exerci tation ullamcorper suscipit lobortis nisl ut aliquip ex ea commodo consequat.

10 point text with 12 points of leading with this line length

Text

In most two-line headings and in some paragraphs, the text itself will affect the leading choice.

Implementation delay causes hollow victory

Negative leading is possible here due to the position of ascenders and descenders which do not overlap

Follow up delays cause hollow victory

Ascenders and descenders overlap, so more leading is required

Test your leading

Once you have arrived at a possible leading choice, try it out on a sample of several paragraphs for your chosen typeface, point size and line length. If it still looks correct, set out a whole page of text, with other possible page elements such as photographs, illustrations, captions, headers and footers, and page numbers to decide if the leading you have chosen works on the page as a whole.

Is the page dark and uninviting or too light so that the text looks as though it will float off the page? Somewhere between these two is the overall page effect you want to achieve.

Spacing between paragraphs

Paragraphs are important divisions within your text. They make it easy for your reader to find their way through the page, and indicate the end of one topic and the beginning of another. Spacing between paragraphs can be used to distinguish these divisions.

This same paragraph spacing can also be used to give emphasis to headings and subheadings.

Paragraph spacing

The computer recognises a paragraph whenever you press the Return key. Using the computer setting you can add a small amount of spacing to the end of each paragraph.

BEWARE

If you are using paragraph spacing, remove one of the two Returns which are often inserted to space paragraphs.

Lorem ipsum dolor sit amet, consectetuer adipiscing elit, sed diam nonummy nibh. Euismod tincidunt ut laoreet dolore magna aliquam erat volutpat. ¶
Ut wisi enim ad minim veniam, quis nostrud exerci tation ullamcorper suscipit. Lobortis nisl ut aliquip ex ea commodo consequat.¶

Only one Return is used to separate paragraphs. No extra returns are used to add space.

Lorem ipsum dolor sit amet, consectetuer adipiscing elit, sed diam nonummy nibh. Euismod tincidunt ut laoreet dolore magna aliquam erat volutpat. ¶

Ut wisi enim ad minim veniam, quis nostrud exerci tation ullamcorper suscipit. Lobortis nisl ut aliquip ex ea commodo consequat.¶

Space is provided by adding space either before or after paragraphs.

Headings and subheadings

The spacing before and after headings can be used to distinguish them from their preceding and subsequent paragraphs.

Euismod

Lorem ipsum dolor sit amet, consectetuer adipiscing elit, sed diam nonummy nibh. Euismod tincidunt ut laoreet dolore magna aliquam erat volutpat.

Aliquip ex

Ut wisi enim ad minim veniam, quis nostrud exerci tation ullamcorper suscipit. Lobortis nisl ut aliquip ex ea commodo consequat.

 Styles, available in most page layout software, ensure consistent paragraph spacing.

Vary the spacing between different levels of headings to indicate the relative importance of these headings. The extra time needed for adding spacing is worth it as it makes your text easier to read and comprehend.

Adipiscing

Lorem ipsum dolor sit amet, consectetuer adipiscing elit, sed diam nonummy nibh euismod. Ut suscipit commodo consequat.
 Duis autem vel eum iriure dolor in hendrerit in vulputate velit esse molesti zzril delenit augue nulla facilisi.

Dolor sit amet

Lorem ipsum dolor sit amet, consectetuer adipiscing elit, sed diam ut laoreet dolore magna aliquam erat volutpat.

Ad minim

Ut wisi enim ad minim veniam, quis nostrud exerci tation ullamcorper suscipit lobortis nisl ut aliquip ex ea commodo.

Indents for paragraphs

Indents on the first line of a paragraph are the traditional way of distinguishing paragraphs. You may choose to use this method alone or together with spacing.

> Lorem ipsum dolor sit amet, consectetuer adipiscing elit, sed diam nonummy nibh euismod tincidunt ut laoreet dolore magna aliquam erat volutpat.
>
> Duis autem vel eum iriure dolor in hendrerit in vulputate velit esse molestie consequat.

Size

The size of the indent should be selected in relation to the length of the text line and to other indents on the page. You can set a smaller indent on justified text than you would for unjustified text.

3 mm indent indicates the start of the new justified paragraph.

Lorem ipsum dolor sit amet, consectetuer adipiscing elit, sed diam nonummy nibh euismod tincidunt ut laoreet dolore magna aliquam erat volutpat. Duis autem vel eum iriure dolor in hendrerit in vulputate velit esse molestie consequat.

Larger, 5mm indent needed to indicate the start of the new ragged-right paragraph. A smaller indent would not show up against the white space at the end of the line.

Lorem ipsum dolor sit amet, consectetuer adipiscing elit, sed diam nonummy nibh euismod tincidunt ut laoreet dolore magna aliquam erat volutpat. Duis autem vel eum iriure dolor in hendrerit in vulputate velit esse molestie consequat.

Don't indent all paragraphs

As indents are used to distinguish paragraphs, there is no need to include an indent on paragraphs which follow a heading, restart the text after a quotation or follow bullet points:

Lorem ipsum dolor sit amet, consectetuer adipiscing elit, sed diam nonummy nibh euismod tincidunt ut laoreet dolore magna aliquam erat volutpat.

Duis autem vel eum iriure dolor in hendrerit in vulputate velit esse molestie consequat —

"nonummy nibh euismod tincidunt ut laoreet dolore magna aliquam erat volutpat sed diam nonummy nibh euismod tincidunt ut laoreet dolore magna erat volutpat"

Duis autem vel eum iriure nibh euismod tincidunt ut laoreet dolore aliquam erat volutpat.

Lorem ipsum dolor sit amet, consectetuer adipiscing elit, sed diam nonummy nibh euismod tincidunt ut laoreet dolore magna aliquam erat volutpat.

- Duis autem vel eum iriure dolor in hendrerit in vulputate velit esse molestie consequat.

- onummy nibh euismod tincidunt ut laoreet dolore magna aliquam erat volutpat sed diam nonummy nibh euismod

Duis autem vel eum iriure nibh euismod tincidunt ut laoreet dolore aliquam erat volutpat.

Bullet points and their indented text need careful positioning in relation to the main paragraphs. More advice on setting bullet points is provided on pages 138–139.

Spacing within titles

When you enlarge text it is often necessary to adjust the spacing between the individual letters. This adjustment is called kerning and is usually applied to text of 18 points or larger.

Kerning aims to create an even optical spacing to the letters in the words and phrases of your titles and subheads.

HANDY TIP

Kerning and tracking are not available in all page layout software packages. Look up 'kerning' and 'tracking' in the Help files to find out.

Better yet

This text has no kerning adjustments

Better yet

Kerning adjustments affect the internal spacings but not the overall line length

Although you add or remove spacing by working with individual pairs of letters, it is the overall even spacing of the letters in the whole word or phrase that you are aiming for.

Practice kerning on text (by following the steps opposite) which you use regularly at large sizes, such as the organisation or company name, to see how you can improve the look of these words and phrases.

Good Company Ltd
Good Company Ltd

Kerning amounts vary, depending on the text size

Power challenges

1 To start kerning, decide which letters are well spaced (not touching and no large white gaps around them). Identify one of these pairs. Spacing here is the average that we will aim for.

Power challenges

2 Now look for letter pairs which have too much space around them, and pairs with too little space between them.

 Give all headings and subheads the same spacing treatment. If you kern one, you must kern all. This provides visual cohesion to the page.

Power challenges

3 Place the cursor between loose letters and remove some of this space with the kerning controls. Add space between tight letters.

Power challenges

Continue until you have adjusted all the necessary letters. You will need to print the page to be sure that the spacing is correct since it is difficult to see the effect accurately on screen.

Spacing within text

Sometimes you will need to add or remove the same amount of space between all the characters and words of your text. This is called tracking.

The addition of space will lighten the look of the page, while the removal of space will darken the page. You are aiming for an even 'colour' to the page so that the headings stand out, but not too strongly and the paragraphs have a middle colour (not too dark or light). The amount of tracking will vary for different fonts and point sizes.

As you look at pages of text, decide for yourself if they are dark or light in 'colour'. This will help you get a feel for adjusting your own text.

Tourism

Tourism is an important industry throughout Britain. It provides jobs for over 1 million people and there is room for further growth. More leisure time, early retirement and more discretionary income mean that more people are going on two or three holidays a year. The industry expects to be the largest employer in the world by the end of the twentieth century.

No tracking is applied to this heading and paragraph. Both show tight spacing.

Tracking can change the look of text. If this happens, you have altered the tracking too much.

Tourism

Tourism is an important industry throughout Britain. It provides jobs for over 1 million people and there is room for further growth. More leisure time, early retirement and more discretionary income mean that more people are going on two or three holidays a year. The industry expects to be the largest employer in the world by the end of the twentieth century.

This heading (Times New Roman, 12 point) has a tracking value of 0.06 applied to it.

This paragraph (Times New Roman, 11 point) has a tracking value of 0.03 applied to it.

Tracking is also commonly used to avoid widows and orphans. These are headings left on the previous page or column, and paragraph ends pushed over to the next page or column.

This extra word is left over at the top of the new column. Tracking for this paragraph is 0.03 as on the previous page.

Tourism

Tourism is an important industry in Britain. It provides jobs for over 1 million people with room for further growth. More leisure time, early retirement and more discretionary income mean that more people are going on two or three holidays a year. The industry expects to be the largest employer in the world next

century.

Overseas market

British tourism faces competition from the overseas holiday market. Many people now travel abroad for their holiday, although the number of people choosing to go abroad for their holiday depends on a variety of factors including exchange rates and the current political situation.

Changing the tracking to 0.02 will move the word back into the previous column and reconnect it with the paragraph.

Tourism

Tourism is an important industry in Britain. It provides jobs for over 1 million people with room for further growth. More leisure time, early retirement and more discretionary income mean that more people are going on two or three holidays a year. The industry expects to be the largest employer in the world next century.

Overseas market

British tourism faces competition from the overseas holiday market. Many people now travel abroad for their holiday, although the number of people choosing to go abroad for their holiday depends on a variety of factors including exchange rates and the current political situation.

Spacing text in presentations

Readers need a lot of help in understanding heading levels in slide and overhead presentations. Place text carefully in the projected area and be sure to maintain spacing accurately between slides.

Features
Two colours
Red
Green
Two shapes
Square
Round

Spacing alone does not bring out the hierarchy

Indentation will help distinguish heading levels. Always kern large text to improve its appearance.

Features
Two colours
Red
Green
Two shapes
Square
Round

Spacing and indents do bring out the hierarchy

Spacing text in reports

Build a hierarchy of spacing for your reports starting by applying the smallest spacing between paragraphs and bullet points. Remember: if you indent paragraphs, you do not need to space paragraphs. So if you have a complex document with a lot of heading levels, choose to indent paragraphs and reserve spacing for the headings only.

More than qualifications ———————————— 3mm space after

Some jobs will continue to require formal qualifications, but a consistent theme that runs through specifications for a job is interest in and commitment to the work, and talent. ———————— 2mm space after

The people who gain jobs in the industry will:

- watch a lot of film and television
- be critical of their viewing ———————— 1.5mm space after

People who work in the industry often 'live and breathe' it. The money is often not great and the hours are very long.

Longer lines require more space to indicate the same levels. Always try out the spacing on a whole page to see if you have the right amount and how it works with margins, illustrations, captions and other space taking elements.

3mm space after ————— More than qualifications

2.5mm space after ————— Some jobs will continue to require formal qualifications, but a consistent theme that runs through specifications for a job is interest in and commitment to the work, and talent.

2mm space after ————— The people who gain jobs in the industry will:

- watch a lot of film and television
- be critical of their viewing

1.5mm space after ————— People who work in the industry often 'live and breathe' it. The money is often not great and the hours are very long.

Spacing text in posters

Space is very important to getting your message across in posters. Readers have to understand the text at a glance. Use spacing between paragraphs with a change in alignment and position to indicate the relative importance of the text.

Much Ado About Nothing

Theatre in the Park
July 7 -12
7.30

Tickets
£5.00, £7.50, £12.00

This event is sponsored by
your local arts authority.

You will find it easier to space out the text in advertisements and posters in small increments if you type each block separately. You can then move them around as independent elements and adjust their position by very small amounts using the mouse. This is quicker than using the paragraph spacing controls, in this instance.

Chapter Five

Organising your space

Good design is about making the best use of the space on your page. Dividing the space into a grid will help you organise it. You will find it easier to mix words and pictures effectively.

What are grids?

Grids are intersecting, non-printing lines which divide the space on your pages into consistent areas.

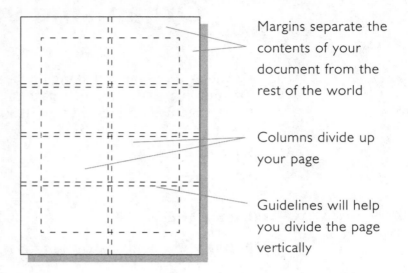

Margins separate the contents of your document from the rest of the world

Columns divide up your page

Guidelines will help you divide the page vertically

Grids provide a framework in which to place your words and pictures. Using them to place material gives your pages a similar look so readers feel that the pages belong together. Using the same grid for a series of reports means that each one will look related to the others.

HANDY TIP

Grids will help you design pages which look as though they come from the same publication.

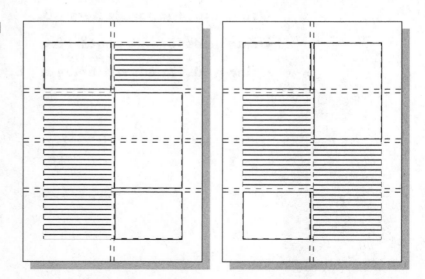

Different types of documents use different grids. Here are two examples of documents, their grids and how they are used to organise text and pictures:

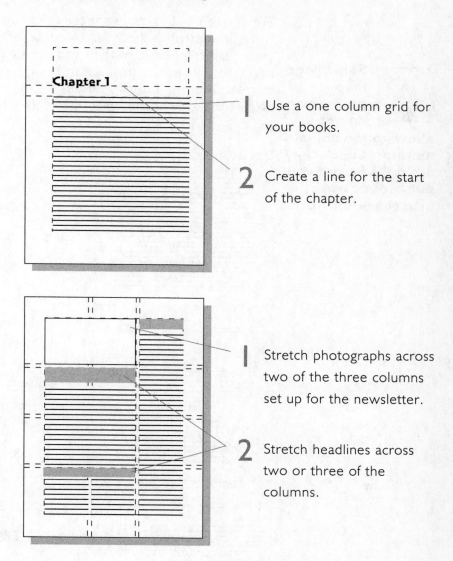

1 Use a one column grid for your books.

2 Create a line for the start of the chapter.

1 Stretch photographs across two of the three columns set up for the newsletter.

2 Stretch headlines across two or three of the columns.

Margins

Margin guides define the top, bottom, left and right edges of the page which separate the words and pictures from the rest of the world.

We are so used to seeing these areas that we give them little thought, but their relative size affects the way that your reader looks at your information. For example, wide margins give an impression of luxury and calmness while narrow margins indicate urgency. The type of document affects the size of the margins relative to the rest of the page.

 Some page layout programs do not allow you to adjust margins. Check they are right before you put a lot of work into the publication.

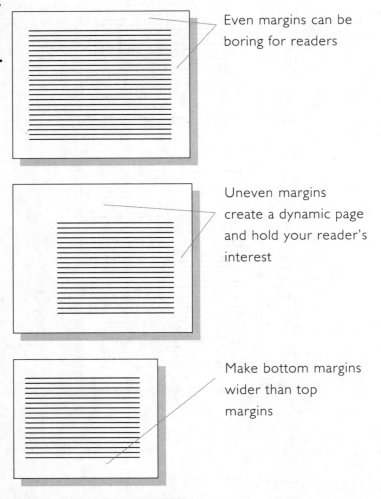

Even margins can be boring for readers

Uneven margins create a dynamic page and hold your reader's interest

Make bottom margins wider than top margins

The left and right margins of pages need different treatment depending on whether you will print the document on both sides of the paper (creating facing pages) or only on one side. If you create facing pages, then you will have inner and outer margins. In this case, the inner margin is less than the outer margin so that the two facing pages look like a single unit.

 You may need to allow space, for the binding of your document, in the left margin for a single-sided document or the inner margin for a facing pages document.

Left and right margins for advertisements and other single page documents are usually even.

Margins for advertisements should be as wide as possible to separate your message from the other advertisements

Columns

Column guides organise vertical areas within the margins for the words and pictures. The number of columns you choose will depend on:

- the type of document you are creating;
- the size of the page;
- the length of line you want.

Reports usually have only one column, while some books and most newsletters use two or three columns.

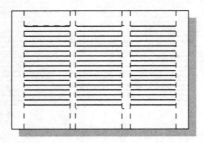

| The simplest approach to using columns is to set up the number you want and to use each one as a single column.

2 A more complex approach is to set up three or more columns and then use them in a variety of ways. This approach provides you with a variety of arrangements which you can mix and match to suit the text and pictures, while still achieving the consistency that grids provide.

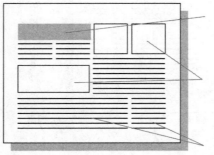

Headlines across two columns

Pictures in one column, or stretched across two columns

Text stretched across one, two and three columns

Guidelines

Guidelines are additional horizontal and vertical lines which you can add to a grid for occasional use. In books, for example, they are used to create a consistent starting position for each section or chapter.

 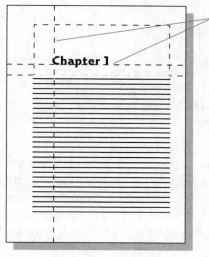

The vertical and horizontal lines ensure consistent placement of the title and start of the chapter

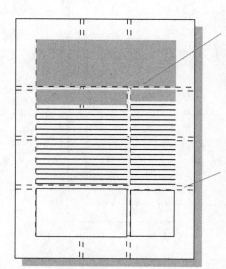

Check on how your page will look when printed by hiding the gridlines. You'll be surprised how different the pages look without the guides.

In newsletters, guides can be used to ensure consistent positions for parts of the magazine.

Guideline indicating the end of the newsletter banner on the first page is used to position pictures on subsequent pages

Double guidelines used to indicate the end of one element and the start of a lower element

Setting up a grid

Once you have decided what type of grid you want to create you are ready to start sketching it out on a sheet of paper.

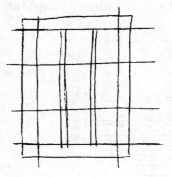

Draw in the margins first and then the columns, and finally any additional guidelines you may need

Now you are ready to transfer the grid to the computer software which you are using for page layout. Refer to the Help files or the appropriate book in the 'in easy steps' series if you are not sure how your page layout program adjusts margins, creates columns and adds guides.

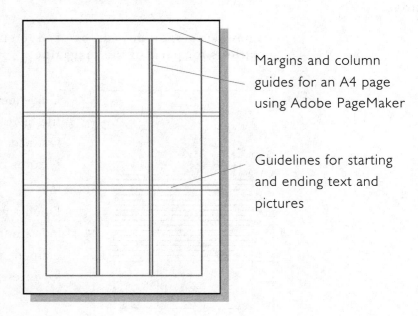

Margins and column guides for an A4 page using Adobe PageMaker

Guidelines for starting and ending text and pictures

...cont'd

Here is an example of a grid set up for an A4 poster to be displayed on a notice board.

Don't make your grids too complex at first – two or three columns and a single horizontal line is sufficient. Build up gradually to more complex grids.

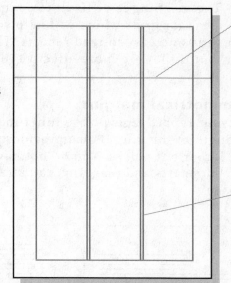

Horizontal guide is used to place the title consistently for a series of similar advertisements

Column guides can be used to align text

Using grids for reports

Reports are read for the information they contain and not usually for enjoyment. Reports can be difficult to read because the words are densely packed and arranged in long lines. The meaning is difficult to comprehend. Here are some ideas for grids which will help you create more interesting and easy-to-read reports. They may use more paper, but if they are more effective the extra paper is worth it.

Asymmetrical margins

Give your report page a large inner margin. This reduces the length of the line. It also provides you with an area to place important points. You do not have to use it all the time, but charts and diagrams can stretch the full width of the page.

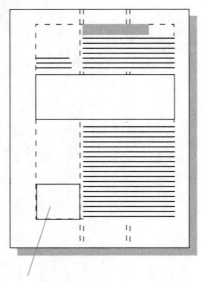

The single column can be used for captions and smaller pictures

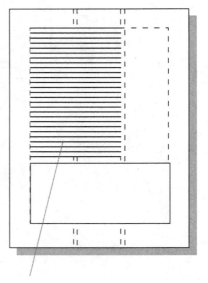

Two columns for the text reduces the line length to a correct width for comfortable reading

Title pages

The design of title pages often bear no resemblance to the design of the report itself. Text is centred on the page and little thought is given to its vertical position. Try taking the title page guidelines from the text pages of the report.

 Uneven margins make your pages more interesting. Using only two columns automatically gives your page asymmetrical interest.

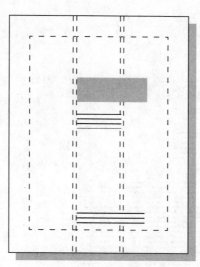

Using two columns from the three column grid visually links the title page to the rest of the report

Using grids for newsletters

Newsletters are composed of several very different page types: short news items, longer articles and listings of events. Each page type should have its own grid. This helps readers find their way through the news to the parts that interest them and to recognise the different sections from issue to issue.

Left and right margins should be even for the front page.

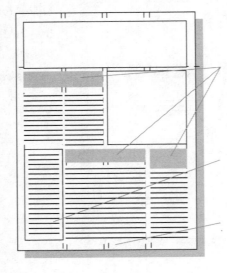

Front page grid

Four columns allow you to start up to three articles on the front page

Contents can be placed in a single column

Use the wider bottom margin for the page numbers

News page

Four columns allows you to fit more short articles into the news page.

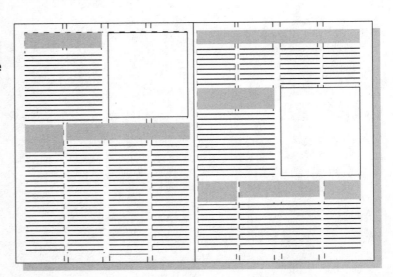

Article page

Readers will spend more time reading the article pages. Line lengths can be longer so a two column grid would be more appropriate for these pages.

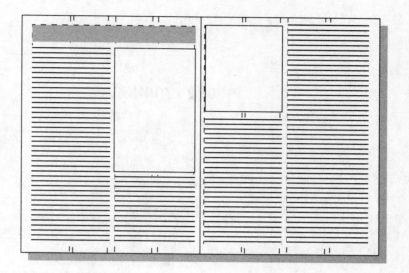

Listing pages

Four or five columns can be used for listed events.

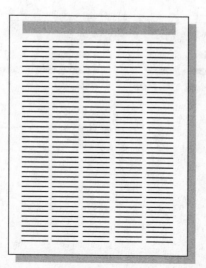

You will need to reduce the size of the type so that the words fit comfortably in the narrower columns

Align this type to the left – this allows uneven line endings which avoid hyphens

Using grids for web pages

Although a very different medium from paper pages, web pages still benefit from the organisation supplied by simple grids. They can help divide the screen into areas used for similar purposes and in this way guide viewers through the web site.

Side bar

Columns

Clustered around an intersecting cross

 Don't use a variety of grids within a single web site. Aim for one grid which can accommodate the content of most of your pages.

Using grids for advertisements

The high cost of advertisements ensures that your aim is to place a lot of information into a small space. Organisation of information is very important. The reader needs to see quickly what you require or have for sale.

Margins
Your advertisement will be placed with many others, so use the margins to make it stand out on the same page.

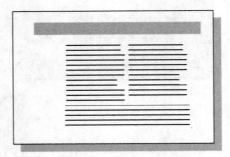

If you have very little space, use one column and margins as wide as you can.

Grid lines are very important to help you space out the text. They can give subsequent advertisements a similar look, helping you to create an advertising house style for your organisation.

Grids and typography

The interaction between the layout grid and the spacing within your text is an important aspect of the overall design of your publication. We can now look at how grids and typography work together.

Chapter Six

Columns and line lengths

Line length is an important attribute in determining whether text is easy to read. The number and position of columns on the page determines the length of each line. The point size will decide the number of characters in that line. Aim to have between 50 and 75 characters per line (include the spaces between words) as this makes for comfortable reading.

Adjust the point size for the column width. Use small type for narrow columns.

Placing fonts in categories enables you to make sense of the vast choice now available and makes selecting a font easier. Categories were initially based on the historical ...

Times New Roman, 12 points

Placing fonts in categories enables you to make sense of the vast choice now available and makes selecting a font easier. Categories were initially based on the historical development of the typeface, but later came to be based on the letter shape.

Times New Roman, 9 points

Rules

Vertical rules can help delineate columns, especially those with left-aligned text. Keep them thin and make sure they are of equal lengths and equally placed in the gutter.

Use Copy and Paste to ensure rules are the same length.

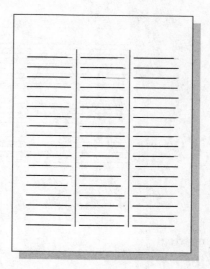

Make sure your text blocks are accurately lined up across columns using guides pulled from the rulers of your page layout program.

Placing fonts in categories enables you to make sense of the vast choice now available and makes selecting a font easier. Categories were initially based on the historical development of the typeface, but later came to be based on the letter shape.

Old style
These types were created between the fifteenth and the mid-eighteenth century. The difference between thick and thin strokes of the letters is subtle as the thin lines tend to be heavy and the curved strokes slope to the left.

Your page layout program offers 'magnetic' guides which help place text blocks into alignment with the column guides. Use this facility to ensure your text blocks are positioned correctly.

Symmetry and asymmetry

A symmetrical design is internally balanced. Each element has an equal opposite. Symmetry represents formality and traditional values. Pages following this style can sometimes seem dull.

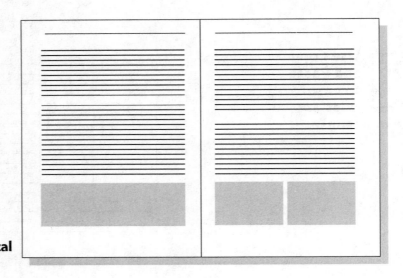

BEWARE

Symmetrical designs can restrict your options in fitting text and graphics into the grid.

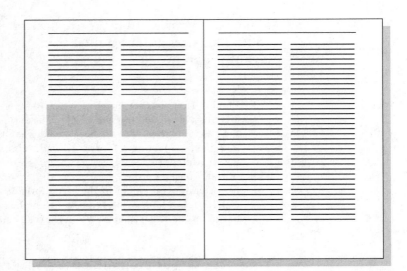

Asymmetrical design is not internally balanced. Elements are unequal and unpaired. The focus is away from the centre of the page. Balance is achieved by juxtaposing graphics and text. Asymmetry represents action and modernity, but take care the design does not overpower the message.

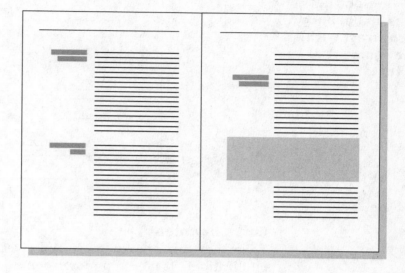

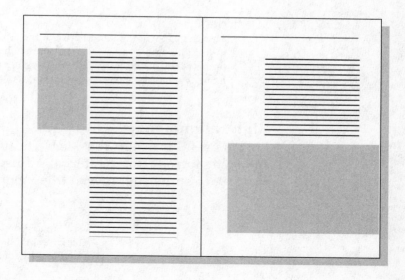

Alignment

Alignment is the positioning of text and graphic elements in relation to each other.

REMEMBER

The alignment of graphics on the page can enhance (or contrast with) the alignment of the text.

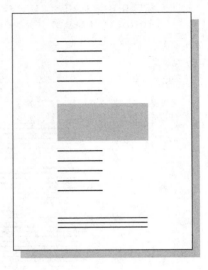

Left alignment

This alignment is easy to use and gives an informal feel to publications. It takes up more room than justified text.

> Old style
> These types were created between the fifteenth and the mid-eighteenth century. The difference between thick and thin strokes of the letters is subtle as the thin lines tend to be heavy and the curved strokes slope to the left.

Right alignment

This is useful for short text such as captions, pull quotes and some introductory material. Adjust line endings to avoid word splits and uneven line lengths.

> Old style
> These types were created between
> the fifteenth and the
> mid-eighteenth century.

Centred alignment

This alignment is of limited use. Restrict it to short pieces of text, or decorative prose. It is difficult and tiring to read as readers have to 'find' the start of each new line.

Old style
These types were created between the fifteenth and the
mid-eighteenth century. The difference between
thick and thin strokes of the letters is subtle
as the thin lines tend to be heavy and the
curved strokes slope to the left.

Old style
These types were created between the fifteenth and
the mid-eighteenth century. The difference between thick and
thin strokes of the letters is subtle as the thin lines tend to be
heavy and the curved strokes slope to the left.

Justified alignment

A traditional formal setting which imparts authority to text. Take care with the length of line and hyphenation. Check word and letter spacing for gaps and tight lines:

Old style
These types were created between the fifteenth and the mid-eighteenth century. The difference between thick and thin strokes of the letters is subtle as the thin lines tend to be heavy and the curved strokes slope to the left.

Don't apply force justified alignment to continuous text, or to short headings in wide columns.

Force justified alignment

This alignment forces lines to stretch the full width of a column. In continuous text, it causes wide spaces in that last line of the paragraph. Apply this setting to headings to space them to fit a column:

Old   style
These types were created between the fifteenth and the mid-eighteenth century. The difference between thick and thin strokes of the letters is subtle as the thin lines tend to be heavy and the curved strokes slope to the left.

Hyphenation

Automatic hyphenation uses either dictionaries or algorithms (sets of rules) to decide where to place hyphens.

Do not allow hyphenation in headings.

Broken words

Either method gives incorrect or poor word breaks at times so hyphenation usually needs careful correction.

Some dictionaries have entries for the correct hyphenation of words. Usually, words should have at least two characters before the hyphen and three after the hyphen. Words with five or fewer letters do not hyphenate.

You should correct hyphenation at the end of your work on the document and always add discretionary hyphens. These will disappear if the line reflows and the hyphen is no longer needed.

> The uncertainty of free-lance earnings and often unsocial hours may represent impos-sible barriers for people with regular financial commitments.

Avoid too many hyphens in a row. One by itself is best, two are acceptable. Never allow three or more as this causes readers to loose their way back to the beginning of the line.

> Many people entering the industry are young with few fin-ancial and personal responsibilities. The uncertainty of free-lance earnings and often unsocial hours may represent impos-sible barriers for people with regular financial commitments.

> Many people entering the industry are young with few financial and personal responsibilities. The uncertainty of freelance earnings and often unsocial hours may represent impossible barriers for people with regular financial commitments.

Changing hyphenation settings will affect the amount of text you can fit on one page and the number of pages in your document. Decide on hyphenation settings early in the design process. Leave only minor corrections to the end.

No hyphenation

You may prefer no hyphenation. Try this only with centred or left and right aligned text. Justified columns require hyphenation to avoid erratic word spacing.

Many people entering the industry are young with few financial and personal responsibilities. The uncertainty of freelance earnings and often unsocial hours may represent impossible barriers for people with regular financial commitments.

Many people entering the industry are young with few financial and personal responsibilities. The uncertainty of freelance earnings and often unsocial hours may represent impossible barriers for people with regular financial commitments.

Left aligned text

Checking and altering hyphenation in left aligned text will give a smoother outline to the right edge of the column. This adjustment will improve the overall appearance of the text and make it easier to read. A similar adjustment will improve right and centred text.

Many people entering the industry are young with few financial and personal responsibilities. The uncertainty of freelance earnings and often unsocial hours may represent impossible barriers for people with regular financial commitments.

Many people entering the industry are young with few financial and personal responsibilities. The uncertainty of freelance earnings and often unsocial hours may represent impossible barriers for people with regular financial commitments.

An awkward gap in the column is corrected with the addition of a hyphen

Grids, spacing and typography in reports

The grid design for reports needs to work with a variety of text across a range of pages. Develop a flexible grid: be prepared to test it with the text on a few pages and adjust it if necessary.

Headings in wide, left side margins help readers find relevant sections quickly and easily.

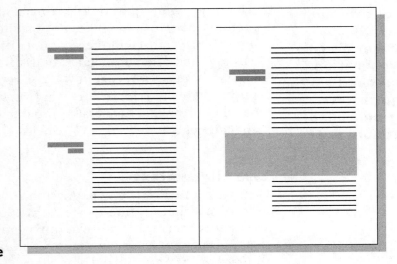

Putting headings within the main text allows you to mirror the facing pages and create wider columns for the main text. Extend graphics into the margins.

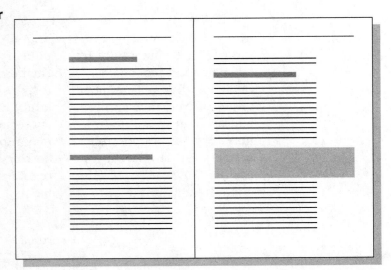

Readers need help to find their way quickly through reports. Section breaks and summaries should be positioned and designed to clearly stand out from the rest of the document. Use bold typography to emphasise the change of report content. The text of headers or footers should change to reflect the section.

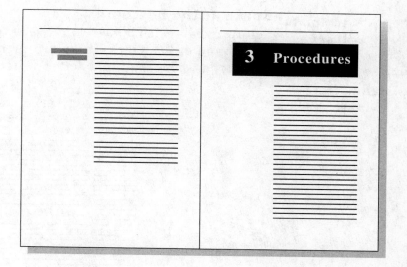

Grids, spacing and text in newsletters

Newsletters are amongst the most complex documents you will design and produce. With a range of articles, a complex text structure (16 or more styles are common) and tight production schedules, you will have many design decisions in every issue. You need a layout grid which will work quickly and efficiently with any text and from issue to issue.

A template will save you time and ensure consistency from issue to issue.

Space at the bottom

Set up a grid which allows you to leave differing spaces at the bottom of the page. Fitting text precisely takes time and does not always result in a better design.

Headings

Align newsletter headings to the left. Keep the same typeface but vary the point size to use up or give you more space on the page. Do not introduce too much contrast in size between the body text and its headings as this makes the pages rather startling to readers.

Introduction

An introductory paragraph provides a smooth visual transition from the title into the article itself. It usually supplies a summary which also helps readers into the article.

HANDY TIP

The italic form of the main typeface is an appropriate choice for the short introduction.

How to change your outlook

Neuro Linguistic Programming (NLP) may be familiar to you in a training context, but what is it and how can you get involved. The idea is that the true meaning of communication is the response we get. Ben Bradley explains the complexities in this first of a series of articles.

Subheadings

Adding short subheadings will break up long articles. This makes the page more interesting and the article easier to tackle.

Cover designs for reports

Keep the design of covers for reports clear and simple. If the report needs a lot of information to distinguish it, place this on the inside title page and leave the cover uncluttered. All that is required is the title, author or publishing authority and the date.

HANDY TIP

The back cover is a good location for less essential (but relevant) information.

Standards of
competence

Issuing
Authority

Date

Avoid punctuation

Don't use colons or full stops. Pick out phrases by placing them on separate lines.

Competence: Standards
for the publishing
industry.

Issuing Authority.

Date.

Competence
Standards for the
publishing industry

Issuing Authority

Date

Illustrations, photographs and graphic elements on the cover encourage people to pick up the report. A captive audience (those who have to read the report) becomes more receptive with an interesting cover.

 Simple line drawings and solid silhouette shapes can be scanned. These do not have to be *directly* related to the content of the report.

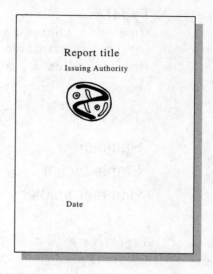

Titles and spines

Binding methods for reports often result in a document without a spine. This makes it difficult to find on a shelf. Place the title along the back cover to compensate for this.

Table design

Tables present complex and often extensive data succinctly and compactly. They require considerable thought and inventive design. Test them on colleagues to see if your ideas enable them to read the table easily.

Typeface

If possible, choose a compact typeface. This will help you get more information in the available space and leave more space for adjusting column widths and row heights.

Tool	One day	2nd day	One week
Hammer	10.00	8.50	24.00
Staple tacker	4.00	2.00	8.00
Hammer stapler	10.00	5.00	20.00

Typefaces with characters which can be confused with numbers should be avoided. Helvetica, Arial and Garamond are examples of typefaces with distinctive number shapes.

1 2 3 4 5 6 7 8 9 0 —— Helvetica

1 2 3 4 5 6 7 8 9 0 —— Arial

1 2 3 4 5 6 7 8 9 0 —— Garamond

Always use lining numbers since these are designed to line up across columns.

1 2 3 4 5 6 7 8 9 0 —— Non-lining numerals in the Bembo Expert font

1 2 3 4 5 6 7 8 9 0 —— Arial's lining numerals

The row and column headings need short or abbreviated text. If you have to extend over two lines, indent or space to ensure that the row headings are easily distinguished.

Text usually aligns to the left, numbers to the right.

Area	Conservation Plan Estimate	Alternate Estimate based on recent visitors to Britain
Africa	657.98	634.87
Asia	200.01	188.07
Europe	450.87	345.98
North America	234.98	298.76
South America	348.87	346.98
Australia	456.53	456.98

Turn headings

Alternatively, you could turn headings. This is particularly useful for tables with long single line headings and short single figure column entries.

Age range	World	Developed regions	Less developed regions
0 – 14	24	18	26
15 – 65	66	63	66
65+	9	19	8

Tables are self-contained units. Distinguish them from the rest of the document by a change of typeface, placement, orientation, rules or a box. Apply these chosen attributes consistently for every table in your document. Readers will develop a familiarity with the way your tables are laid out and find them easier to understand.

REMEMBER

Tables should be numbered through the document and provided with a caption.

Tool	One day	2nd day	One week
Hammer	10.00	8.50	24.00
Staple tacker	4.00	2.00	8.00
Hammer stapler	10.00	5.00	20.00

Avoid a cell grid

You do not have to add a grid of lines to delineate the table cells. The alignment of data in rows and columns will create the grid.

Tool	One day	2nd day	One week
Hammer	10.00	8.50	24.00
Staple tacker	4.00	2.00	8.00
Hammer stapler	10.00	5.00	20.00

Compare this table to the one above it. The cells do not help the reader to understand the information; they merely divide up the table.

Rules

Horizontal rules can help readers scan across table columns. This can be particularly useful if the columns are widely spaced or some of the cells are left empty. Use rules to group entries under columns and subcolumns. Bands of grey can also be used to distinguish rows across columns.

 HANDY TIP

Varying the weight of lines will help distinguish different parts of data.

Tool	Day rates		
	One day	2nd day	One week
Hammer	10.00	8.50	24.00
Staple tacker	4.00	2.00	8.00
Hammer stapler	10.00	5.00	20.00

Tool	One day	2nd day	One week
Hammer	10.00	8.50	24.00
Staple tacker	4.00	2.00	8.00
Hammer stapler	10.00	5.00	20.00

Preliminary pages

Many documents contain information relating to their production, printing and distribution. In books, these preliminary pages (they are usually placed at the front) contain the definitive title, information about the publisher and publication date. Other information can also be included. If the document is long enough it will contain a table of contents and may include a list of figures.

Title page

Title pages can be illustrated, but most designs rely on typography for their impact. It is not necessary to use the same typeface as the book itself, since the choice should work well at large type sizes.

Draw the design of these pages from the grid and layout of the rest of the book

HANDY TIP **Design these pages last in relation to the rest of the publication.**

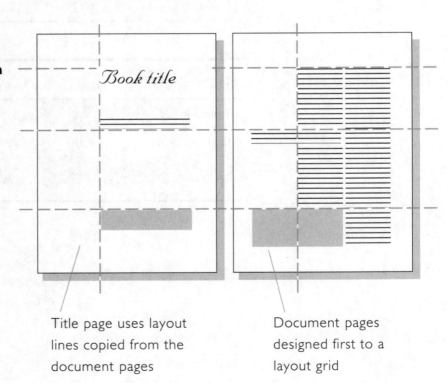

Title page uses layout lines copied from the document pages

Document pages designed first to a layout grid

The remaining pages should be treated as a group and, although they may be designed individually, should give a sense of cohesion. Usually the same typeface is used as in the book.

Copyright page

This page contains an indication of copyright ownership, year of publication, notice of liability, trademarks and the International Standard Book Number (ISBN).

Table of contents pages

Created last, this page lists the chapter/section titles with their corresponding page numbers. You may want to include subheadings from reports where this will help readers find their way through a complex document.

Avoid dotted lines designed to help the reader find the correct page. These are not always necessary and give your pages an old-fashioned look. A better approach is to place the page number in front of the entry or place it close after:

1 Introduction	**1**
Title and Date of Commencement	3
Objectives	3
Implementation of the Procedures	4

1	**Introduction**
3	Title and Date of Commencement
3	Objectives
4	Implementation of the Procedures

Slide presentations

Slide presentation materials are read under unusual conditions. Keep in mind these circumstances when creating your design.

Poor conditions

Readers will view the slide for a limited time under less than optimal conditions (bright screen, darkened room). Choose a highly legible typeface. Use size and space rather than a change of face to distinguish parts of the text.

> ## Scanners
>
> Resolution
> Speed
> Cost

No return

Readers cannot return to the slide at will to check their understanding. Limit the amount of information on each slide, use a clearly defined typeface and create a simple structural hierarchy based on size and indents. Two levels are optimal in addition to the title.

> ## Resolution
> Dots per inch
> 300 dpi
> 600 dpi
> Pixels per inch
> 150 ppi
> 300 ppi

One of many

An individual slide is only part of what could be a long presentation. A simple grid provides continuity, but avoid graphic elements like logos repeating on every slide. These take up precious space and quickly become boring.

<table>
<tr>
<td>

Cost

Quality
Time for scan
Options

———————— Scanners Ltd

</td>
<td>

Lines can help define the edges of the slide, but be careful they don't take up space better used for the information

</td>
</tr>
<tr>
<td>

Options

Software
Free delivery
Slide scanning

———————— Scanners Ltd

</td>
<td>

The company logo is best left on the first and last slide of a presentation and not added to every slide

</td>
</tr>
</table>

Taking note

Provide your audience with print-outs of your slides (in reduced format) so that they do not need to take extensive notes in a darkened room.

Using templates

Templates are files which allow you to base one document on another. They maintain consistency in style and save time by using similar, standardised graphic elements and text across a range of documents.

What to keep in templates

Keep these aspects of a newsletter in the template:

REMEMBER

Template files are distin- guished from documents in your computer by their icons or file extensions. Keep them together in a template or folder for quick access.

- The layout grid

- The typographic styles

- The page types which make up the newsletter

- Repeated graphics such as logos and banners

- Information about the publisher, organisation and staff

Create all the parts of a document which will be common to the series. (This might include the styles, page layout grid, position of headers and footers, and page numbers.) When you are satisfied you have added everything, save the document as a template.

Open the template when you are ready to start a new document. All the design work is then ready in the new document and you can be sure that it will closely resemble all the other publications in the series.

Chapter Seven

Spice up your design

Special effects will sustain your readers' interest in long documents and gain their attention in single page publications. Used consistently across a range of publications, they will help to build a recognisable style.

Rules

Rules are lines which, positioned in relation to your text, can increase a reader's understanding of your message. Variation in line width, value and style offer a wide range of rules for you to use.

Look here

Look here

Rules which relate to text should be added as part of the paragraph attribute.

Look here

Look here

Look here

Look here

There are several advantages to using rules instead of underlining text. Rules sit below the descenders (or above the ascenders) and do not cut the letters' outline, leaving them easy to read.

Peter Piper on the level

Peter Piper on the level

Peter Piper on the level

...cont'd

Rules can extend beyond the text itself, and in this way divide the page into sections.

 Rules intended to appear on all pages should be added to the master pages.

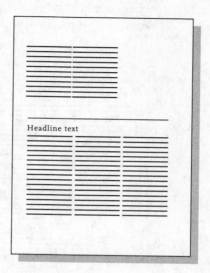

As graphic elements, rules can add contrast and balance to your pages and help define the page area.

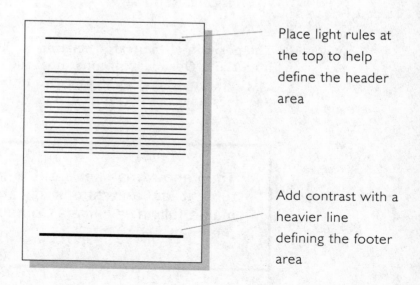

Place light rules at the top to help define the header area

Add contrast with a heavier line defining the footer area

Boxes

Adding a box around text will set the enclosed text apart. As with rules, you can choose from a range of weights, values and styles for the lines. Keep in mind that your choice must work to separate text while fitting in with the rest of the page. Keep the contrast small.

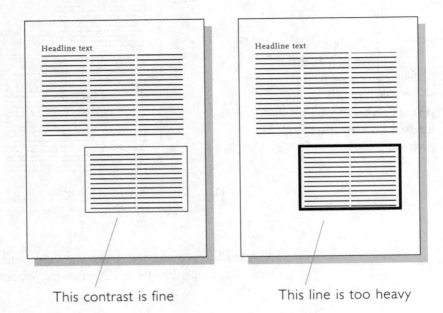

This contrast is fine

This line is too heavy

The position of the text in relation to the line is very important. Obviously, it must not touch the line but take care to keep it far enough away from the line so that the text does not appear cramped.

> The canoe was like a leaf in the current. It took it up and shook it, and carried it masterfully away, like a Centaur carrying off a nymph.

Restrict your boxes

Too many boxes on one page or a double page spread will confuse the reader. Create one main focus on each page with a single box.

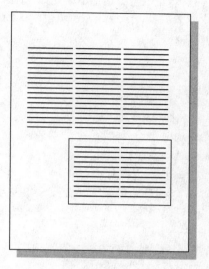 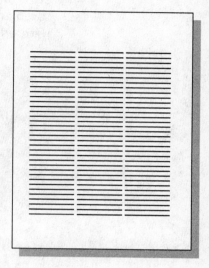

Tint panels

Tint panels can be used as an alternative to boxes or in conjunction with them to offer a contrasting background.

Setting text against tints

Text must remain readable when set against a tint. Make sure the grey is light enough to maintain a contrast with the black letters, or dark enough to maintain a contrast with white letters.

We took to the paddle with good hearts, like people who have sat out a noble performance and return to work. The river was more dangerous here; it ran swifter, the eddies were more sudden and violent.

This contrast is strong enough to leave the text easy to read.

 Use typefaces and type styles with clear outlines and large counters against tints.

We took to the paddle with good hearts, like people who have sat out a noble performance and return to work. The river was more dangerous here; it ran swifter, the eddies were more sudden and violent.

This contrast is not strong enough. The text is difficult to read.

Tint panels can be used alone as graphic elements.

Even when you take precautions in setting text against a tint, it is more difficult to read than type set against a white background. Set only limited amounts of text this way.

Pull quotes

Singling out parts of the text for placing between quotation marks (pull quotes) will add interest to your publication. Quotes provide readers with an access point into longer text, by allowing them to read a short piece as they skim the rest. Choose the words carefully to encourage people to read on.

The quoted text block adds interest to the page as a graphic element. Placed consistently, they can lead readers through the pages of a long report.

 If you use a random arrangement, keep the style of the quotation the same.

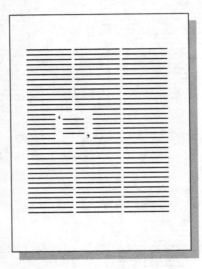

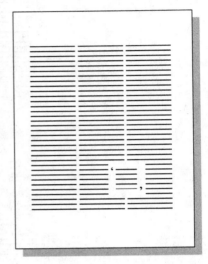

 Readers start looking for quotations placed on every page. This encourages them to read through the document.

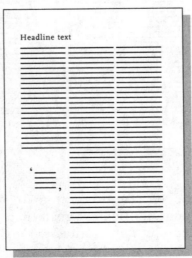

Quotation marks can be either single or double, but whichever you choose, remain consistent within one publication. Lines and enlarged quotes can be used to set them apart.

" Over 40% of businesses read our magazine "

" Over 40% of businesses read our magazine "

'Over 40% of businesses read our magazine'

Alignment and position affect the way pull quotes work with the page design. Positioning quotes to fit into the page grid in the same way that photographs do will give the page cohesion.

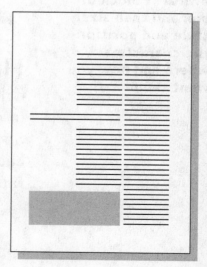

Initial letters

Initial letters (also called drop caps) can be added automatically to paragraphs by most page layout software.

Held every year, the conference brings delegates together from all over the world to celebrate in a beautiful location. Special facilities are provided to encourage delegates to bring their families.

The design options using automatic initial letters are limited. If you have the time, more interesting and appropriate typographic effects can be created.

HANDY TIP **Highlight the letter (or words), cut it from the surrounding text, place it in its own text block or box and then size, style and position the characters where and how you want them.**

Held every year, the conference brings delegates together from all over the world to celebrate in a beautiful location. Special facilities are provided to encourage delegates to bring their families.

Held every year, the conference brings delegates together from all over the world to celebrate in a beautiful location. Special facilities are provided to encourage delegates to bring their families.

You are not limited to using only initial letters; words and phrases at the beginning of paragraphs can be given a different typographic treatment.

THE canoe was like a leaf in the current. It took it up and shook it, and carried it masterfully away, like a Centaur carrying off a nymph.

THE CANOE WAS LIKE A LEAF in the current. It took it up and shook it, and carried it masterfully away, like a Centaur carrying off a nymph.

THE canoe was like a leaf in the current. It took it up and shook it, and carried it masterfully away, like a Centaur carrying off a nymph.

Where and when

As with all these effects, don't over do it. Initial letters provide emphasis to the first paragraph, but avoid applying initial letters to all paragraphs.

The effect is most often seen in magazines, illustrated books and newsletters. Because of its association with these publications, they seem less appropriate in a business report.

Bullets

Bullet points, usually added to the start of each paragraph in a group, draw the reader's attention to the list of points. Points are used instead of numbers where each paragraph is of a similar importance.

Bullet size

Most typefaces offer a bullet point character designed to fit with the rest of the letter shapes. You may want to reduce the point size.

- larger objects appear closer

- lighter colours bring shapes closer

- larger objects appear closer

- lighter colours bring shapes closer

Bullet shape

You may want to use a different bullet. ITC Zapf Dingbats and Wingdings, a typeface provided with Microsoft products, will offer a range of bullet shapes. You will definitely want to change the size of these shapes so that they do not dominate the text.

- ❄ larger objects appear closer

- ❄ lighter colours bring shapes closer

- ❖ larger objects appear closer

- ❖ lighter colours bring shapes closer

Adjusting text

Bullets need several typographic adjustments to ensure the text reads smoothly. Make sure you adjust the size of the indent from the bullet to the text and indent any follow on lines.

The landscape can be divided into three main types

- mountain ranges which make up the central core of the country

- peninsulas which jut into the oceans on either side of the country

- coastal plains which vary in width and offer low rainfall

Sentence structure

You will also need to decide whether the bullet is part of an on-going sentence or whether each bulleted point represents a complete sentence. Use one style only throughout a single publication and adjust punctuation.

The landscape can be divided into three main types.

- Mountain ranges which make up the central core of the country.

- Peninsulas which jut into the oceans on either side of the country.

- Coastal plains which vary in width and offer low rainfall.

The landscape can be divided into three main types:

- mountain ranges which make up the central core of the country,

- peninsulas which jut into the oceans on either side of the country and

- coastal plains which vary in width and offer low rainfall.

Reversing text

White text against a black background provides a strong contrast with the remaining text and graphics. Reversed text is more difficult to read, so select only words or short phrases and choose typefaces with bold and clear letter shapes.

> The canoe was like a leaf in the current. It took it up and shook it, and carried it masterfully away, like a Centaur carrying off a nymph.

 Check the effect of these strong graphic elements on the page as a whole.

Reverse headings

Top level headings and section divisions can work well in reversed text.

 Look here   Subheading

Try reversing text against other letter shapes:

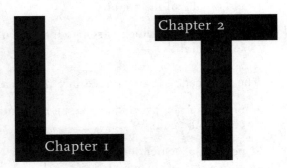

Rotating text

Rotated text is difficult to read. People usually turn their head on one side, to read it without rotation, so limit the amount of text you turn at an angle to the page. Rotating text effectively indicates section divisions. The rotation provides an interesting contrast, and the short text makes it easy for readers to grasp its meaning.

If you place text at an angle, keep the degree and direction of rotation the same for all rotated text in the publication.

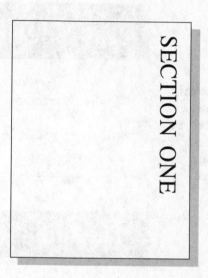

Words and phrases should be rotated as a complete unit. Reading characters from top to bottom is tedious. This effect will attract more attention than the text needs.

```
V   T   I   H   T   R
E   E   S   A   O   E
R   X   R       R   A
T   T       D       D
I
C
A
L
```

Mixing these effects

Adding more than one of these effects to a page or within a document needs careful consideration. Their graphic quality means they can compete with each other, leaving readers confused. Try combining effects in one graphic element.

Section One

 HANDY TIP

Use a mix of these effects to create strong divisions between report sections.

Posters need dramatic effect to draw readers' attention, so you can use stronger contrasts, but these must work together and result in one clear emphasis.

Business seminar

The Inflationary Universe

Thursday, 10.30
Meeting Room

For more information call Extension 5647

Avoiding common design mistakes

A small number of problems appear regularly in work by inexperienced designers. This section looks at ways you can avoid these errors.

Chapter Eight

Using emphasis effectively

Readers need guidance in understanding the structure of your text. Emphasis is created by contrasting the size, weight, shape, colour and position of headings, body text and other structural text within the document. Taken together, they subtly guide the reader through the document and help them understand the structure.

Posters and display material can accommodate strong contrasts.

 HANDY TIP

Size and space provide the strongest contrast. Change these attributes first for the greatest effect.

Plays in the Park

Wind in the Willows

Alan Bennet

The Children's Playhouse

5-10 August at 2.30 pm

Text on this page shows only a small change of point size and is evenly spaced, leaving little contrast on the page

Plays in the Park
The Children's Playhouse

Wind in the Willows

Alan Bennet

5-10 August at 2.30 pm

Greater changes in text size and more extreme spacing leaves more obvious emphasis which helps readers pick out the important parts of the information more easily

Underlining

Underlining makes the outline of words difficult to see. It is as commonly used for emphasis as capitals and should also be avoided. Use rules for emphasis instead.

<u>Typography</u>

Underlining cuts through the descenders of the word

Typography

Rules allow the word outline to be read and can be varied in weight

Continuous text

Emphasis in continuous text requires careful consideration of the balance of the page as a whole. Text should remain easy to read and contrasts should not distract readers' attention. All emphasis should be seen against the background colour of the page. If you are not sure whether you have the balance correct, ask a colleague to look at the page(s).

Look at the changes in emphasis in this book to see the range which is used. The page headings and subheadings are designed to stand out against not only the continuous text, but also against the varied illustrations which are used.

In this book, the Handy Tip, Remember and Beware text is strong enough to be picked out easily. The text used in captions for the illustrations has much less emphasis since it is already easy to pick it out from the main text from its position on the page. Also, it is designed to be seen in relation to the illustrations and not to appear too dense alongside these graphics.

Work your typefaces hard

If you have a complex text structure, you may find that you will need to add another typeface to bring out this complexity. However, make sure you explore all the possibilities of your first typeface before adding new ones.

Bold

An obvious possibility is the addition of bold. All typefaces have a single bold which will appear to bring about a change in point size, and which can be used to create the impression of several text levels.

Lorem ipsum

Lorem ipsum

Lorem ipsum

Lorem ipsum

Semi-bold (available in some purchased typefaces) provides a more subtle alternative to bold.

Small capitals

Use of small capitals, with bold and italic, will extend your choice. True small capitals are supplied by the purchase of an additional typeface, usually called an expert font.

LOREM IPSUM

LOREM IPSUM

LOREM IPSUM

LOREM IPSUM

Building a range of typographic styles
Here is a range of typographic styles with the
corresponding text from a booklet or business report, using
one typeface.

 **Changes in
point size
of 0.5 are
enough to
distinguish some
parts of your text.**

Section heading — Times New Roman, 24pts

Page numbers ———————— Times New Roman, 12pts,
(Bold)

Body text ———————————— Times New Roman, 11pts

Quotations ———————————— Times New Roman, 10pts

Pull quotes ———————— Times New Roman, 12.5pts

Add in another typeface and you have additional
possibilities for other parts of the document.

Captions ———————————— Helvetica, 10.5pts

Headers ———————————— Helvetica, 12.5pts

Choose appropriate typefaces

Typefaces are designed for a particular purpose. The letter shape, weight, stress and other attributes affect the way the typeface works. Matching these attributes to the functions of the text in a document takes skill. Also, you may not have a wide range of typefaces to choose from.

Get to know your typefaces

If you have followed the advice in Chapter Three, you will have created a sample paragraph and alphabet of each typeface on your computer. Look carefully at each list and get to know their characteristics. Now divide your catalogue of typefaces into categories based on the following criteria:

- *Best size:* Some typefaces are appropriate for setting at small sizes (eg, setting catalogues and directories), some are better suited for display (eg, in posters) and some are best used at a size appropriate for reading continuous text (eg, books and other literature). Decide which of your typefaces are suited to small sizes, display and continuous text.

- *Compactness*: Some typefaces can fit more letters into a given length of line than others. This compactness is decided by the width of the individual letters and the amount of spacing each letter and word receives. Some typefaces are redesigned to offer a compact setting. These are usually referred to as condensed or narrow and are appropriate for narrow columns such as in newsletters or tables.

This is Gill Sans at 24 points
This is Gill Sans Condensed at 24 points

- *Plain or elaborate:* Some typefaces, even those with serifs, have a simple letter outline. Others have elaborate swashes, complex and unusual letter shapes, or look as though they have been written with a pen. Use these for invitations and special effect on posters, but avoid their use in continuous text or tables.

A script typeface may look lovely but it is difficult to read

Helvetica's plain, simple letter shapes carry your message and do not detract from it.

The simple serif face of Times New Roman will work well at a variety of sizes.

Using capitals

People commonly place titles and headings in capitals thinking that it gives them emphasis and helps them stand out. Unfortunately, capitals are difficult to read because they make words without distinct outlines.

TYPOGRAPHY

A rectangular word outline gives little help to the reader

Typography

Irregular outlines help adults to recognise words

Sentence case

Headlines and headings are sometimes typed with each of the important words given emphasis with a capital letter. This technique does not really add the intended emphasis since the additional capitals are distracting. It would be better to use sentence case, where only the first word is capitalised.

Will the Millennium Ever Be Over?

Capitals at the start of words can be distracting to the reader

Will the Millennium ever be over?

Reserve capitals in headings for those words which are correctly capitalised

Small caps

Small capitals which offer smaller letter size in a capital letter shape can offer a pleasing contrast with upper and lower case text. The word outline is still obscured so you should only use them in small text blocks.

WILL THE MILLENNIUM EVER BE OVER?

Spacing capitals and small capitals

If you do find a use for capitals, you should always add spacing to the words – otherwise the letters will appear too close together.

WILL THE MILLENNIUM EVER BE OVER?

No additional spacing

WILL THE MILLENNIUM EVER BE OVER?

Spacing adjusted

Effective use of alignment

Centred alignment

Centred alignment is a common choice for displayed text. As it is also seen in older forms of printing, such as title pages of old books and old posters, centred alignment conveys a sense of traditional, old-fashioned values. Use centred alignment only if these are the values and approach you want to convey.

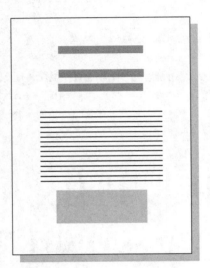

Centred alignment is appropriate for the title page of a book or report. It gives a sense of order and authority, but can appear dull and undynamic.

Right alignment

Right aligned text is difficult to read and can be tiring in long passages. It can be very effective in small amounts of text and in short lines and can be used to distinguish text from other blocks. Right aligned text adds contrast to the page.

This is where the path ends and the climbing begins. Here, rugged determination is needed to pull through the tough onslaught of boulders and ice.

Since right aligned text is difficult to read, hyphenation should be avoided and you should take care over line breaks.

Mixed alignment

Mixing alignments in a document or on one page should be handled carefully. Readers can be distracted by the different alignments and the mix can make the page seem confused.

 Print out thumbnail diagrams of your pages to get a sense of how the text positions look throughout the document.

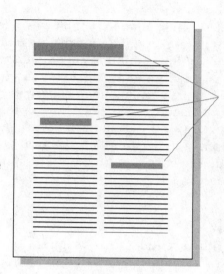

Even these simple pages have an uncomfortable look with the main heading aligning to the left and the subheadings showing a centred alignment.

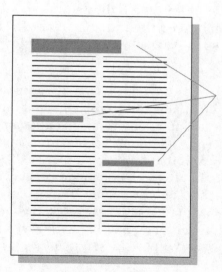

Using the same alignment for both the main heading and the subheadings simplifies the page and emphasizes the alignment on the page as a whole.

Effective use of bullets

Bullets are used frequently to visually separate and emphasise a group of points from the body text. If you carry out the following extra work on them they will carry your message more effectively.

Lorem ipsum dolor sit amet, consectetuer adipiscing elit, sed diam nonummy nibh euismod tincidunt.:
- ut laoreet dolore magna aliquam erat volutpat ut wisi enim ad minim veniam, quis nostrud
- exerci tation ullamcorper suscipit lobortis nisl ut aliquip ex ea commodo consequat
- duis autem vel eum iriure dolor in hendrerit in vulputate velit esse molestie consequat, vel illum Dolore eu feugiat nulla facilisis at vero eros et accumsan et iusto odio dignissim qui blandit praesent.

Indent

Indent the second and subsequent lines of the individual points. This allows the bullet to stand out more clearly. Set the indent to the position of the text of the first line. You can also indent the bullet points themselves, but this is less essential. Keep the indents small. If the gap is too large the bullet seems detached from the following text.

Lorem ipsum dolor sit amet, consectetuer adipiscing elit, sed diam nonummy nibh euismod tincidunt:
- ut laoreet dolore magna aliquam erat volutpat ut wisi enim ad minim veniam, quis nostrud
- exerci tation ullamcorper suscipit lobortis nisl ut aliquip ex ea commodo consequat
- duis autem vel eum iriure dolor in hendrerit in vulputate velit esse molestie consequat, vel illum Dolore eu feugiat nulla facilisis at vero eros et accumsan et iusto odio dignissim qui blandit praesent.

Avoid using too many bullet points in your text. They become less effective when used frequently.

Spacing the bullets from the main text

Add spacing between the main text and the group of bulleted points. This helps distinguish the points when looking at the page as a whole and is useful to the reader who is trying to refer back to a section of text quickly.

Lorem ipsum dolor sit amet, consectetuer adipiscing elit, sed diam nonummy nibh euismod tincidunt:

- ut laoreet dolore magna aliquam erat volutpat ut wisi enim ad minim veniam, quis nostrud
- exerci tation ullamcorper suscipit lobortis nisl ut aliquip ex ea commodo consequat
- duis autem vel eum iriure dolor in hendrerit in vulputate velit esse molestie consequat, vel illum

Dolore eu feugiat nulla facilisis at vero eros et accumsan et iusto odio dignissim qui blandit praesent.

There is more information about setting bullets correctly on pages 122–123.

Diagonals

Diagonals are strong design elements but should be used carefully. Beginners setting out to distinguish lines of type placed below each other in displayed text often indent them. This creates a diagonal line from the end of each line of type.

Lorem ipsum
Dolor sit amet
Consectetuer adipiscing
Elit sed diam

These indents should be avoided as they create a diagonal which adds nothing to the readers' understanding. It is better to place lines of type under each other against a straight vertical.

Lorem ipsum
Dolor sit amet
Consectetuer adipiscing
Elit sed diam

Diagonals can be used effectively to pick out small amounts of text, but it is better to include the diagonals as a graphic element and then place the text against it.

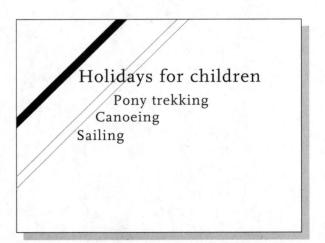

Chapter Nine

Graphics in your designs

Well-placed, carefully selected graphics will improve your publications. They add to your readers' understanding of the text and make your pages more interesting.

Covers

Improving your pages with graphics

Photographs, diagrams and graphs, drawings, cartoons, and logos will all help your readers understand your message. How you use them, where they are placed and the way you present them will determine how effective they are.

Gather all your graphics together at the beginning of the design process.

Choose photographs carefully

Photographs should be chosen to enhance the message and not detract from it. This is not always easy unless you can commission a professional photographer to record events. Try to build your own collection of photographs about your company or organisation and keep it up to date. Ask enthusiastic amateurs to use their cameras. Unless you plan to publish in colour, specify black and white photographic prints as these will give a better quality when printed in black and white.

Aim for a consistent style

As the compiler of a publication, you may be provided with a range of diagrams, graphs and charts from different sources. You must make sure the style of each of these is consistent. This means the typefaces should be consistent and that labelling, titles and legends should be in the same position, same typeface, point size and writing style.

You may have to commission an illustrator to redraw the diagrams from the source material in order to get the pages consistent.

Flat artwork and digital files

Flat artwork, drawn using traditional drawing and painting techniques on paper and card, is still the most common way illustrations are created. This artwork is then scanned to put it in electronic form. An alternative method is to use illustration software to create the files directly.

A computer stores, displays and prints graphics in a variety of formats. These formats work in different ways and affect the changes you are able to make when designing and laying out your publication. If illustrations are presented as electronic files, check you know which format they are in. There is more about formats on pages 148–149.

There is more about scanning and formats on pages 152–155.

Cartoons

Humour in print should always be handled carefully. Badly drawn and unfunny cartoons detract from, while good ones add an extra dimension to, your message. Commission a cartoonist to draw them, but don't indicate too closely what you want. Provide them with the text and ask them to decide what would be humorous.

Working with logos

Logos are the graphic representation of a company or an organisation. The specially designed graphic is intended to be easily recognised and help readers recall quickly the company it represents and what it stands for or sells.

Know the rules

Many companies maintain rules about how to use their logo. Placement, colour and size may be decided for you.

Design in your logo

Your document design will need to consider how the logo will be included. Work it into the design so your pages reflect its influence, rather than work against it.

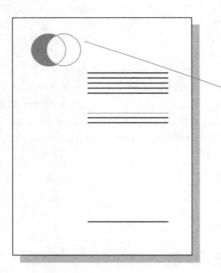

The soft, round shape of the logo contrasts well with the elongated, rectangular shape of the text on the design for this report page.

Colour and size

If you have to print the company logo in colour you may need to use a very specific ink. Some companies provide printers with the ink they must use for the logo. Others specify the colour from a colour library. Some logos vary depending on the size they are printed. In some cases, the company name is included within the logo when it is used at a larger size. Check the rules on colour and size.

Fonts and logos

If a logo includes text, the font is specified and usually included in the graphic file. However, some companies leave the choice of fonts in documents to the author/designer/producer. Make sure you select a font which complements any text in the logo and works well with the logo itself.

Resizing

You will often want to change the size of a logo. If the graphic format is an Encapsulated PostScript (EPS) you will be able to alter the size without affecting the quality of the printing. If the file is a bitmap file, making the logo larger will reduce the quality of printing. For this reason, logos are often in EPS format – if you have the choice you should request the file in this format.

Preprinting

Where a logo requires colour and most publications are printed in black and white, some companies arrange for A4 sheets to be preprinted with the logo. This is an economical way of including the coloured logo. If you are using preprinted paper, set up a template which takes into account the position of the logo. This will enable you to quickly add text in the remaining spaces on the page.

Working with clip art

'Clip art' describes the small images which are often dotted liberally around newsletters. These graphics can add sparkle to your newsletter and document pages, but take special care in selecting and placing them.

Free libraries with software packages

Most clip art used in office documents is provided free with word processing and graphics software packages. These images can be bland, and, as everyone knows that they are free, their liberal use can give an impression of amateurism.

Other sources

If you find you need to make extensive use of clip art for your newsletter, or for posters, consider buying one of the clip art packages. These usually provide more interesting drawings and some are genuinely humorous.

 Choose clip art with a similar look for a single document or newsletter issue. Do not vary the style through the document as this will make the pages seem scattered.

Another rich source of small images are the copyright free books which provide black and white graphics. These can be scanned as needed. Some could appear regularly in your publications while others could be used for specific articles.

Be sure the clip art does enhance the page. If in doubt, leave it out. White space is better than a poor graphic.

Other possibilities

Your clip art does not need to illustrate points in the articles. You could add it to provide contrast on your page. The black and white image will provide an excellent foil to the grey of the text.

Illuminated letters

Illuminated letters can be added to the beginning of articles. They draw attention to the start of the piece as well as provide a contrast to the text. These devices would be appropriate for newsletters and brochures, but they are unlikely to enhance the feel of a business report. Letters can be scanned from copyright free books.

Small printing devices

Most computer systems offer a font which provides small symbols. Add these to your pages to separate articles in newsletters or to indicate the end of a section in a longer report. PC computers call the font Wingdings, while Macintosh computers call the font Zapf Dingbats.

Graphics formats

Computer graphics are created in two different formats. These formats affect how you are able to work with the graphic in the page layout program. For example, vector graphics can be resized without any printing problems, while bitmap graphics may not print well if they have been enlarged.

Bitmapped graphics

Bitmapped graphics are created and stored as information about the small individual pixels which mix together to build up the picture. Think of them as a mosaic made up of small squares of tile.

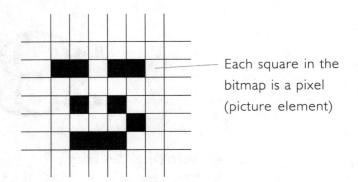

Each square in the bitmap is a pixel (picture element)

In black and white bitmaps, each pixel is described by one bit of information. This means the pixel can be either black or white. A greyscale bitmap requires eight bits of information to describe each pixel. The various combinations available from eight bits of information make it possible to describe 256 different shades of grey from white through to black. Coloured bitmaps can also be described using 8 bits of information. The more bits of information used to describe each pixel, the larger the file.

The most common type of bitmapped graphic is a Tagged Image File Format (TIFF). On the PC computer, the extension for this type of file is .tif. Other file types include the Windows Bitmap which uses the extension .bmp and the Graphics Interchange Format (.gif).

Vector graphics

Vector (or object-oriented) graphics are created and stored as mathematical descriptions of the points and curves used to delineate the image. The most common type of vector graphic format is an Encapsulated PostScript format (EPS).

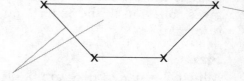

The position of points on the image are described by x and y values

The lines joining the points and the colours and patterns filling in the shapes are described mathematically

 If you are unsure of the format of a graphic, look at the dialogue box displayed when it's imported to your document. The format will be shown here.

HANDY TIP

Graphics in page layout programs

When you import a graphic file into a page layout program, only the part of the file which is used to display the image on screen should be added. Adobe PageMaker gives you the option of importing the entire file, QuarkXPress only imports the screen file. The larger part of the file is required for printing and the software program keeps links to this file. If any of the files are moved, the link is broken and must be updated. Both software packages offer controls to update links.

Although page layout software offers controls for resizing, rotating and cropping graphics, it is better to perform these operations in graphics manipulation programs designed to carry out these tasks. Import your graphics files already cropped, rotated and sized.

Line drawings and diagrams

Line drawings, diagrams and charts can come from a variety of sources. Authors often supply rough sketches. Sometimes diagrams and charts are supplied from other computer programs such as spreadsheet packages. You may be able to use some of these, but many will need to be redrawn. Redrawing ensures that all diagrams in the publication are consistent in style. This is important as it gives cohesion to the report and authority to the information.

Size

Adjust the size of diagrams to fit with the rest of the page. Do not let charts overwhelm the text, but make sure they are large enough to show the data easily.

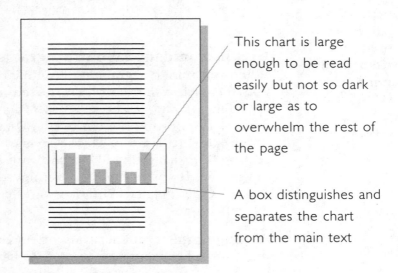

This chart is large enough to be read easily but not so dark or large as to overwhelm the rest of the page

A box distinguishes and separates the chart from the main text

Fonts

Choose ones which are the same as in the text, or which contrast and work well with the text. Compact typefaces will enable you to fit in more label text.

Format

EPS formats are usually the best for diagrams and illustrations if they are created using computer programs, as files in this format can be resized without affecting the final print quality.

Labels

Labels should be succinct, clear and appropriate. Always include units for charts and diagrams. Sometimes the information can be included in the body of the chart.

A graphic representation is more memorable than text.

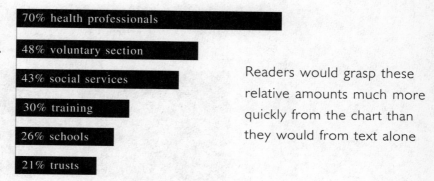

Readers would grasp these relative amounts much more quickly from the chart than they would from text alone

Sometimes a legend is necessary. This is usually added when the information is too complex to label individually. Legends require the reader to put in more effort to understand the information, so make them simple and distinguish the different items as clearly as possible.

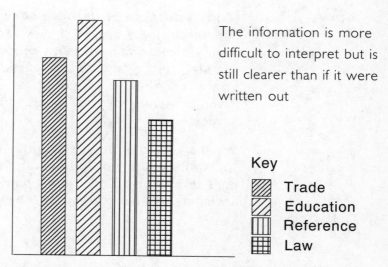

The information is more difficult to interpret but is still clearer than if it were written out

Book sales in first quarter for various sectors

How scanning works

Photographs and artwork are converted to digital computer files by a scanner. A light source is projected on to the original image. Light of varying intensity and wave length is reflected back onto light sensitive diodes which convert the light into electrical impulses. These are then recorded.

A close look at a bitmap file shows the individual squares which make up the image.

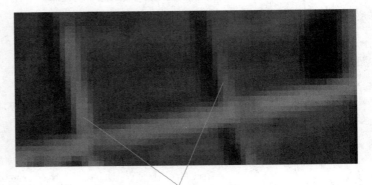

This is a close up of the ribs inside the boat on page 156

Do it yourself or using a service bureau

Low resolution scanners (below 1200 dots per inch) are standard equipment in many offices. Use these scanners if you are printing at 600 dots per inch on the office laser printer or below. If a higher printed quality is important, or if you are using transparencies as originals, use a service bureau.

Service bureaus offer a scanning service. They will provide you with the low resolution scans and your printer with the high resolution scans. Your cropping and resizing decisions will be retained by the substituted files.

There are several aspects to scanning which need to be carefully considered and resolved before talking to a service bureau or scanning originals yourself.

Half-tones and resolution

Scanning resolution is the number of times the scanner samples the original in an inch. The half-tone is the number of screen lines per inch for the printer. There is a relationship between the two – the scanning resolution should be twice the half-tone screening frequency. If you are planning to alter the size of the scanned image, use this formula for deciding on your scanning resolution:

BEWARE

Scanned image files can be large. You may need to upgrade your computer system to use them effectively.

$$\frac{\text{Final image height}}{\text{Original image height}} \quad \times \quad \text{screen ruling} \quad \times \quad 2 \quad = \quad \text{scanning resolution}$$

If you don't know what the screen ruling is, then ask your printer.

Scanning mode

Scanners can be set to record black and white, greyscale and colour pixels. Choose black and white for line drawings, greyscale for black and white photographs and colour for any colour photographs or coloured art work. Once you have scanned the colour, you can alter and improve the colour balance in image manipulation programs.

File size

Scanning results in large graphic files. A small colour photograph can easily be over 5 MB in size. Large files take up storage space and can be difficult to work with. Keep your file sizes as small as possible by scanning only the parts you will use, at the lowest possible resolution for quality printing, and by choosing the correct scanning mode.

Working with scanned images

Unless you have commissioned art work to a specific size, you will want to alter the original images so that they better suit your document.

Cropping

Cropping removes parts of the image and prevents them from printing. Page layout programs allow you to crop images, but the part of the image which is removed remains in the file and continues to take up storage space. It slows down the work you do with the rest of your document. Ideally, cropping should be done at the scanning stage or when you work with the image in the image manipulation program.

Resizing

Resizing after scanning alters the resolution of a bitmap image. For example, if you have an image which measures 1 inch by 1 inch, with a resolution of 300 samples per inch and you stretch it so that the image is 2 inches by 2 inches, the resolution becomes 150 samples per inch. (The 300 samples per inch are stretched over two inches instead of one inch.) Image manipulation programs can restore the resolution but they do this by making up pixels. This process is called interpolation. Interpolation is never as good as resizing the image at the scanning stage.

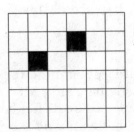

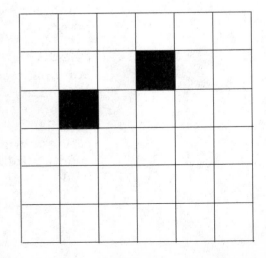

Manipulating the image

Scanned images usually need some form of improvement. Often the scanning process darkens black and white photographs which then need to be lightened. Sometimes the colour balance needs adjusting to remove a red, green or blue hue to the image. All these changes can be done in image manipulating programs such as Adobe Photoshop.

The process requires an in-depth knowledge of the software program and considerable skill in looking at the image, deciding on the changes and then making them to the correct extent. You may want to get help with this process if you are not experienced in this area.

Image as scanned without any adjustment

Image adjusted to improve contrast and brightness

Adding photographs

Choosing pictures

When selecting pictures of people, remember that portraits and action shots engage readers. Try to avoid posed line ups to record events. They are less interesting than people doing something.

HANDY TIP **Crop portraits close to a face, or at the shoulders. Ideally, leave some space above the subject's head.**

Interior shots and buildings need people to set the scale and to add interest. Choose shots which have foreground and middle ground subjects.

Cropping

Most photographs will be improved by cutting away the edges to focus on the important part of the photograph. When cropping photographs of people, avoid cutting across heads and hands.

R H Deahl

Cropping the photograph here will focus attention on the main subject

Background

Middle ground

Foreground

Sizing

One large photograph adds impact to a page and is better than several smaller photographs. If you have to use small photographs to fit them in, group them rather than spreading them around the pages.

Be sure to resize photographs in proportion so that the image is not distorted.

Bleeds

Any photograph or other graphic which crosses the margin of a page and ends at the edge is a bleed. Bleeds provide a strong direction and should be planned as part of the double page spread. It also helps if you can place them with reference to the following and preceding pages.

Include bleeds as part of the page layout and grid of your document as a whole, and not just to a single page.

Adding effective captions

Captions offer you an opportunity to further enhance your readers' understanding and enjoyment of your publication. People often scan a publication before reading it thoroughly, dipping into captions as a way of sampling the text.

Writing captions

Captions create a link between the text and the graphic and should enhance the readers' understanding of both. Try to avoid merely describing what the readers can see for themselves. Write text which adds to the overall interest of the material.

Try
Local sailing clubs offer competition and cruising activities in the sheltered waters of the local bay

Not
Two boats sailing in the calm waters of the local bay

Length

Keep your captions short so that the information can be absorbed quickly and easily. Unless the book text is composed entirely of captions, two or three sentences is usually all that a reader will take in. If you have a lot of information to supply for a photograph, you might consider placing it in a special section at the back of the publication.

Position

Captions should be positioned consistently in relation to the graphic so that the reader knows which caption relates to which graphic. You often see captions underneath, but placed at the left or right side can be equally effective.

Photographs and drawings should be credited somewhere in the publication.

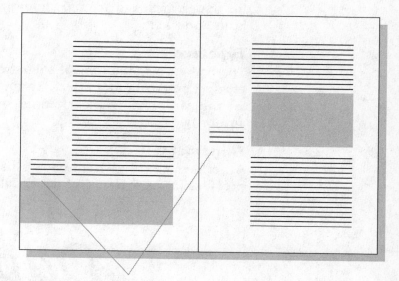

The wide margin of a report is a good position for captions. If you place them in this space throughout the document, they can be placed above, below or alongside the graphic they describe.

Style

The typeface, point size, leading and other aspects of style should be consistent. Italic is a common choice for style with a centred alignment. Although there is nothing actually wrong with this, you might want to choose a style which is less commonly used. This is a place where you could safely change the typeface, possibly to a sans serif style, or use a smaller point size than the main text and change the alignment. In some cases, very short captions could be right aligned.

Banners for newsletters

Banners, at the top of the front page of your newsletter, display the name of the publication and usually include information about the organisation, and the newsletter's volume and date. Although they contain a lot of text, they are usually designed to work as a single graphic. As an advertisement for the publication, the banner should aim for the greatest impact and should remain unaltered from issue to issue.

Typeface
The banner sets the tone of the newsletter, so choose the typeface to create that effect. Script letters give a friendly feeling while bold, dark letters provide an impression of authority.

Alignment
An off-centred alignment gives a lively feel, while centred provides an impression of dependability.

Contrast

Use the banner to create a strong contrast with lighter text on your front page. Reversing the nameplate out of black will provide impact. This effect could be repeated on later pages to add cohesion to the newsletter.

HANDY TIP

Test your designs on some friends or colleagues to see if they produce the effect you want.

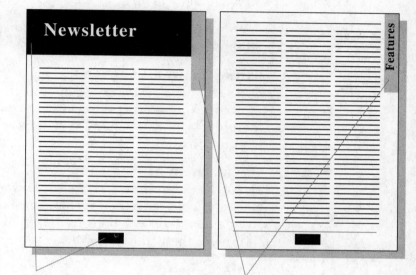

Strong reversed letters in a black banner create interest. The effect is repeated for the page numbers on the inside pages.

Grey side bar provides contrast and a way to indicate divisions within the newsletter.

Checks

There are a lot of details relating to the banner design of a newsletter:

- check on the printing costs for your design

- check the banner design can be read and understood quickly

- check the newsletter contains the correct organisation and publication details, such as date and version number

Managing graphics

The process of creating a document which uses graphics to enhance its communication is more complex than creating a text-only publication. Acquiring, labelling and controlling the archiving of the original work and the graphic files, and ensuring the graphics and the page layout files reach the printer together, all requires considerable project management skills.

Here are some final pointers to managing the use of graphics in your publications.

Bring them all together
Gather all the graphics together at the start of the design process. You will get a much better idea of where the graphics will be used and how they will enhance the communication.

Treat them all the same
Treat all the graphics in the same way. This will create a sense of coherence in your design. For example, if you frame one diagram, then frame them all; if one photograph is tinted, then tint them all.

Think ahead
Build a portfolio of photographs. If you know an event is taking place in your company, then arrange for photographs to be taken. Gather photographs from other sources and maintain an archive.

See what others do
Look at how other publications use graphics. Draw ideas from them. Keep pages from publications which you think will provide inspiration.

Build from black and white
Use black and white photographs or line art in your first publications. Move on to colour when you have used black and white graphics in a few publications.

Tints

Grey shading or tints, placed behind text or as graphic elements, will make your pages more interesting. Unlike true colour, they create contrast without increasing the cost of printing.

Chapter Ten

Adding tints to black and white

Tinted shapes become graphic elements on the page in their own right, but unlike solid black, they provide a gentle contrast to the text. Most page layout programs offer a range of tints of black. The printed results vary with the resolution of the printer.

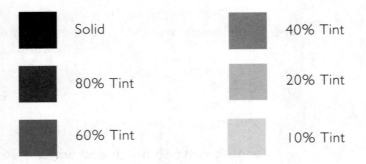

■	Solid	■	40% Tint
■	80% Tint	■	20% Tint
■	60% Tint	■	10% Tint

If you are using a higher resolution printer, create grey tints by taking a percentage of process black as has been done in this book.

■	20% Grey	■	40% Grey

When you start to add tints, choose only one or two of these percentages to work with on your document. With solid black, reversed text and the white page you have many combinations.

Hooray   *Hooray*

Hooray   *Hooray*

Hooray   *Hooray*

One common use of tints is to add a shadow to a text box. Further possibilities include tinting text, lines and other shapes.

The shadow tint raises the box off the page

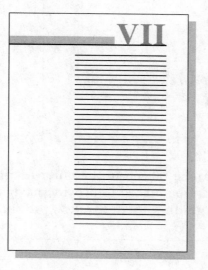

Printing tints

The tints usually become darker when they are printed. If you are printing or photocopying your publication from camera-ready copy from your office laser printer, test the strength of grey tints. If your electronic files will produce film, you should ask your printer about the most effective percentages for shading.

Blends, the grading of one level of tint into another, do not print well on laser printers with less than 600 dots per inch resolution. The higher the resolution the smoother the blend.

Using tints in reports

The main text of a report should be left without a tint so that it is easy to read. Tints can be added to boxes (see page 116) and to the initial pages to provide effective contrast with the rest of the report.

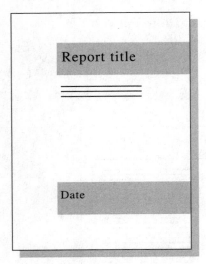

Tints can be placed in the outer margins of report pages. These can be placed to provide navigation aids to the reader, guiding them through the sections of a long report.

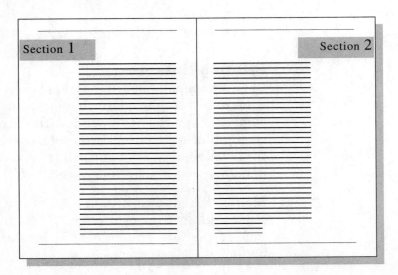

Using tints in posters

Contrasting tints against black and white shapes can add dramatic effect to posters. Select the text or graphic for contrast carefully, to ensure the correct information receives the full benefit of the emphasis.

 Large areas of tints can print unevenly on low resolution office printers.

EFFECTIVE MANAGEMENT

16 JULY

BROOK HOUSE

Cutting
Edge

A report on selling techniques in the household tools division

Using tints in newsletters

Tints can be used effectively in the banner of a newsletter.

REMEMBER

Office laser printers do not print right to the edge of A4 paper. Avoid tint bleeds if using this type of printer.

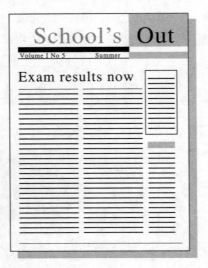

Any tint will make the text more difficult to read, so choose short pieces; contents, listings and short articles are good places to use tints. If you do want to use a tint behind an article which extends over more than one column, use the tint throughout the extent of the article.

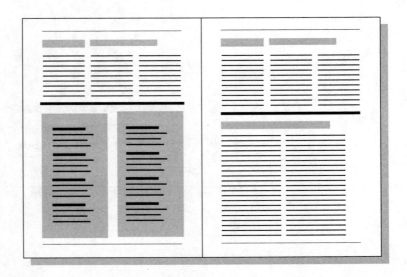

A simple but effective way to add a tint and contrast to your newsletter is to place the page numbers against a tint. You could bleed the tinted shape off the bottom or top edge of the page.

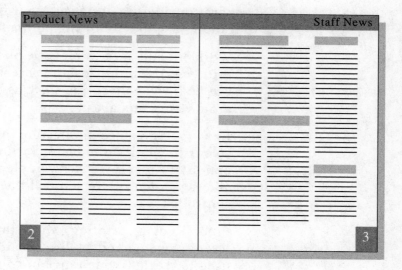

Add tints to graphics. This provides contrast to the text and reduces their visual effect on the page as a whole, which is often stronger than necessary, if printed in black.

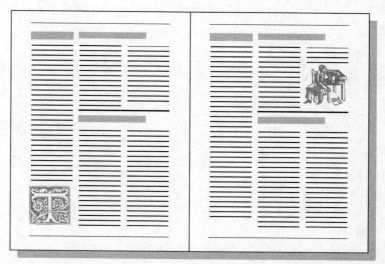

Using true colour

While tints will make your publications more interesting, true colour will transform them. However, adding colour effectively to your designs is complex and colour printing can be expensive.

If you are considering designing your first colour publication, keep the following points in mind:

- Work out and agree a realistic budget and contact a printer early in the design process. A printer's advice can be invaluable at this stage as they will help you avoid costly mistakes.

- In your first colour publication, use one additional colour (in addition to black, for the text). With the option of tints, this gives you plenty of scope and allows you to explore some of the effects of colour in a controlled way.

- Process colour printing, where three coloured inks (cyan, magenta and yellow) in addition to black, are used to create a wide range of colours, is essential if you want to reproduce colour photographs in your publications. You do not have to add any further colour if you are uncertain of its effect. If you do add other process colours to your design, there is no additional printing cost.

Chapter Eleven

Designing web pages

As web-page software becomes easier to use, non-designers will create these new 'publications'. The same design principles apply, but you will need to consider other aspects of the new medium.

Covers

Design principles for web pages

Web pages are viewed on a computer screen. This places restrictions on the design although the basic design principles of spacing, appearance, contrast and balance still apply.

Keep text to a minimum
Make sure your readers can read the text easily and don't give them too much to read. If you have a lot of information, make it easy to print by not including a lot of graphics.

Before you start your design, look at a range of web pages and decide what you like and don't like and what you find easy to use.

The web site for Digital type review has a very simple, direct home page. It downloads quickly.

Navigation
A series of individual pages make up a web site. Make sure your readers can find their way around your web site. Ease of navigation is as important as content if you want your readers to return. All sites have a main or home page which downloads first. This page should give readers an idea of what to expect of the site.

NEWS   REVIEWS   FEATURES   LINKS   INFO   ARCHIVES

The navigation bar for the Digital Type Review offers an immediate entry into any part of the site.

Design for the screen size

Many web sites offer long web pages and expect readers to use the scroll bar extensively to see the entire page. Using the scroll bar is tiring and a long page is a daunting prospect. Ideally, divide your information into topics which can be seen on one computer screen at a time. If necessary, make the page no more than two screen depths. Direct the reader to another page using a button, if you want to add more information than can be held in this area.

The home page for the Computer Step web site fits into a standard size computer screen

Make pages consistent

Consistency in the look, colour and 'feel' of pages is important in web publishing because of the difficulty readers have in keeping track of where they are in the site. Pages which cover the same topic should have a similar look or background colour. Establish and use grids.

Creating and publishing web pages

The basis of web publishing is a text format called HyperText Markup Language (HTML). This format of text file contains the text which you want to display on your web pages along with the coding which tell the browser how to display the text.

```
<TR VALIGN=TOP>
<TD HEIGHT=2></TD>
<TD COLSPAN=5></TD>
<TD COLSPAN=4
ROWSPAN=8><P>This popular
series of five 30 minute films
encouraged all non-mechanics to
tackle their own cars. </TD>
<TD ROWSPAN=8></TD>
</TR>
```

Coding for position, alignment and style

The text which will be displayed on the web page

Graphics

In addition to the text and codes, the HTML file contains references to graphics files which are also displayed and show photographs, background images and additional text in formats which the browser cannot display.

```
<A HREF="/solutions/
photocaption/main.html"><IMG
SRC="GIFShome/
980518caption.gif" ALT="Write
Captions That Roar"
WIDTH=130 HEIGHT=50
BORDER=0></A><BR>
<IMG SRC="/GIFS/
spacer33.gif" WIDTH=3
HEIGHT=5 BORDER=0><BR>
```

Reference to the GIF image

Alternative text which will display if the viewer has the graphics downloading option switched off

Browsers

Browsers are software programs which display the HTML files with the accompanying graphics, sound, animation and video files. When you enter the unique address of the page and the computer storing it, the page is sent to your computer, held there and displayed by the browser. As you click on links in this page, additional pages are sent, held by your computer and displayed on your screen.

Web pages and web sites

One HTML file is required for each web page. Additional pages are provided by other HTML files with their own linked graphics. A web site consists of all the page files, their graphics files and any additional files for sound, film or animation. The page HTML files are linked so that a reader can click on a text link, button or image on one page and display the linked page. Pages can be viewed in any order so readers are no longer restricted to a linear approach when reading your site as they would be with a book; they can quickly jump around to areas that interest them.

Designing text for the web

Understanding technical aspects of web text will help you design appropriately.

HTML text

The look of HTML text is decided by the settings of the browsing software. The designer indicates a text type which is then interpreted and displayed by the browser.

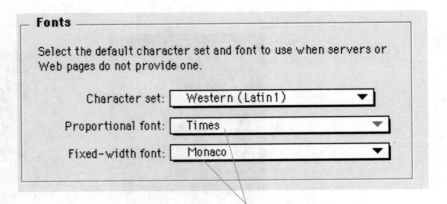

Preference settings in the browser allow readers to decide how the HTML text will look

Styles

Few designers are content to let others decide the look of text. Browser and HTML software developments now provide increasing design control. Styles can now be set which determine more closely how the text will look.

GIF text

Text can be displayed on web pages as graphics. Designers retain complete control over the look of the text and can use the complete range of typefaces. The compact graphic format (GIF) takes slightly longer to download than HTML but many designers feel this is a small disadvantage for the greater control over the design.

On screen text

Reading text on computer screen is difficult and tiring. Give your readers as much help as you can. If you do not take care, readers may get fed-up and leave your site.

Size

Ensure the text is sized to be read easily. Many web surfers leave their browser settings at the default, so you could assume that the sizes you set will be viewed that way.

Line lengths

Avoid long line lengths; they are even more difficult to read on a computer screen. Readers do not like scrolling along to read the entire length of line.

Restrict your line length to between 50 and 70 characters for easier reading.

Text style

Choose styles which give a clean letter outline and avoid drop shadows at the back of your text. If you want a three-dimensional effect, apply shadows to graphics.

Colour

Colour coding indicates web page links. Link text changes colour when the link is followed. If you add colour to your GIF text, remember that these links already add colour to the page, so co-ordinate your new colours with these link colours.

Helping readers navigate

Web sites usually contain many pages. Readers move around using links but this maze can be difficult to navigate. Readers may get lost after viewing a few pages; their time is wasted and they leave your site frustrated.

Navigation routes

Plan routes through your site carefully. A diagram of the pages and the links will help you see if the routes make sense. Once constructed you must test the site extensively to make sure all the links work correctly. Some sites contain a map which gives readers an overview. All web pages should have links which return readers to the main or home page.

Always check web site links carefully before publishing your site.

The index and search links allow readers to search the site quickly

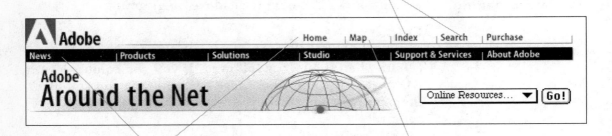

Links to the Home page allow readers to get back to base quickly (they can start their exploration of the site again from this known point)

The map of the site gives an overall view of the structure of the document

Links

Text and graphics can both form links. Some readers prefer to browse without downloading graphics, so your web pages should offer both text and graphic based links. Where readers do download graphics, buttons (graphics which act as links) add colour and interest to pages and direct readers' attention to the links.

News & Features
- Tips
- Case Studies
- Gallery
- Columnists
- Events
- Press Releases
- Back Issues

Text links change colour to indicate that a visitor has used them. They also download with the page and do not require graphics to load to be seen and used.

Special Offer: Acrobat Reader and PDF Writer!

Adobe Experts Make New Book Picks

INSITE Web Content with Context

Graphics links add interest and colour to web pages. They can be fun and enliven the content but require careful design to work well.

Graphics on web pages

The web is a visual medium and no site is complete without graphics to augment the text. Some sites are almost totally constructed from graphics. The balance of text to graphics will depend on the purpose of the site; some sites providing information to visitors will be mainly text, other sites providing entertainment or marketing will depend heavily on graphics for their effect.

 If you are publishing photographs, you should crop the image so that the most important part is emphasised.

HANDY TIP

Museum Opening Hours

The Louvre Museum is open every day except Tuesdays. It is also closed on the following public holidays. In 1997, the 11th of November and the 25th of December, in 1998, the 1st of January, the 12th of April, the 1st of May, the 8th of May, the 31st of May, the 14th of July and the 25th of December. On all other public holidays the museum is open from 9 a.m. to 6 p.m.
Permanent collections: from 9 a.m. to 6 p.m., evening opening hours until 9.45 p.m. on Mondays (short tour), and Wednesdays (the entire museum).
Sale of tickets ends at 5.15 p.m. or 9.15 p.m.
Galleries start closing at 5.30 p.m. or 9.30 p.m.
Hall Napoléon, under the pyramid, is open every day, except Tuesdays, until 10 p.m.
Medieval Louvre and History of the Louvre: from 9 a.m. to 9.45 p.m.
Temporary exhibitions under the pyramid: from 10 a.m. to 9.45 p.m.

The Louvre site provides a lot of information on opening hours in a text heavy presentation

The Discovery Channel web site depends heavily on graphics for its interest and dynamic style

Compression and file format

Any graphics must be provided in as small a file size as possible. There are two main compressed file formats for Web graphics: Graphics Interchange Format (GIF) and Joint Photographic Experts Group (JPEG).

Use thumbnails

Where the image is an important aspect of the content of the page, some sites show readers a small sample of the image. This allows them to preview the image before committing themselves to downloading the full image.

Avoid large graphic files which take time to download. Readers will not wait long and will leave your site.

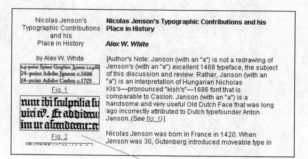

These thumbnails of the images indicate what the readers will see if they choose to download the file

Effective web page backgrounds

Background images

Web pages can display images behind text. This effect is often used but needs to be handled carefully as it can detract from the message. You could use a simple overall pattern which provides colour and texture against which your text can be placed. If you take this approach, keep your text short and simple so that it is easy to read against the background image.

Keep navigation text to a minimum. Reserve long text pieces for actual content and offer readers an opportunity to download longer files in a compressed format for off-line printing.

More complex images can be used if they are placed to one side and combined with a light colour or fade to white.

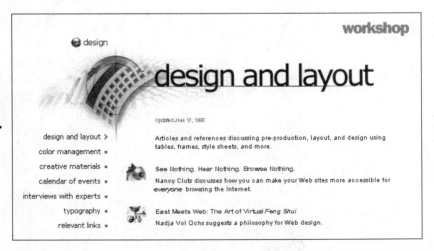

Coloured backgrounds

If you are not sure about using this effect, try applying a plain coloured background to your pages. Dramatic web sites use black, dark grey or white backgrounds.

Black and white photographs look good against a dark background and small amounts of coloured text also contrast well. Additional small splashes of colour and interest can be added with coloured lines. Full colour photographs with one strong colour also provide contrast and drama on your pages.

A black background contrasts well with full colour photographs.

Other content on web pages

One of the most exciting aspects of web sites is that they can communicate with more than just pictures and words. Animated images, sound, film, games and other interactive media can be added to web sites.

Much of this new media is intended to entertain rather than to inform. If these additions are included in informative web sites, they should assist the reader to understand the message, rather than make it more difficult to comprehend.

Animation

Animated images can be added as small files which repeat a cycle of movement. Since readers respond immediately to any movement on the computer screen, animation can so strongly attract the reader's eye that it's difficult to read and concentrate on other parts of the page. Make sure that the animation sequence does add to the web page and is not there just to show you can handle the new technology.

Animation sequences are short and cannot be turned off, so they repeat all the time that the page is displayed. This can become boring very quickly. Before you decide on adding animation, make sure that it will not turn readers away.

If you want to see some of the latest animation files, many of the internet search engine sites hold animation files. Try www.altavista.digital.com or www.excite.com.

...cont'd

Sound

Sound is less commonly found on web sites, although some record company sites offer clips of their latest releases. For these sites, sound is a wonderful addition.

Audio files are very large and take a long time to download so you have to click on the link to download the file rather than have the file load automatically. Most web sites warn readers of the download time before they commit to calling for the file.

Audio files require additional software to play the sound. Streaming technology allows browsers to start playing the sound while still downloading the file, so people can listen to live broadcasts.

If you have the time and want to listen to some digital audio files, you could get to them from www.midi.com

Film

Digital film files can be added to and displayed on web pages with additional software. Again, these files are large and only small clips of film are usually shown.

A good site for film is the Museum of Modern Art in New York at www.moma.org

Editing and addition of sound and film requires considerable technical knowledge. If you feel your site would benefit from the addition of sound or film you will probably need to contact someone with experience in these areas.

Getting and keeping visitors

See the titles Web Page Design in easy steps and HTML in easy steps.

People need to find your site and once found, you want them to return. Make sure you register your site with the main search engines. These can be found through both the main browsers, and most offer registration e-mail.

However, these engines are frequently overloaded so you will also need to publicise your site on all your printed material. Include the address on your letterhead and any other marketing materials.

Update your site regularly

Web sites are a dynamic form of communication. You should keep your site up to date and aim to change it regularly. Knowing that a site changes will keep your visitors coming back. Include a date indicating when the site was last updated. This gives readers the idea that your site is changed regularly.

File management

You will not need to update all the pages on your site. Some will change, while others will stay the same. Good file management and careful control of page file names is very important so that you update and republish the correct files.

Links to other sites

One way to keep people coming back is to offer them links to other sites on similar or related subjects. You can add these links to your web pages, but you should make sure they stay up to date.

Index